HOW TO ...

understand and apply reforms in SEN policy

Lois M. Addy

Thank you for the support provided by my colleagues in Specialist Support, North Yorkshire Local Authority, a SEN Pathfinder, as we face the implementation of the plethora of legislative changes together.

Thank you to my family – Geoff, Bethany and Charlotte – for their patience and flexibility, which has enabled me to complete this project.

Thank you to Juliet West for her perseverance in editing this book so that it is accessible to teachers and parents alike.

How to understand and apply reforms in SEN policy

ISBN: 978-1-85503-568-3

© 2014 Lois M. Addy
Illustrations by Becky Pinniger / Shutterstock / NYCC SpLD Service / DfE / Ian Tovey.

This edition published 2014
10 9 8 7 6 5 4 3 2

Printed in the UK by Page Bros (Norwich) Ltd
Designed and typeset by Andy Wilson for Green Desert Ltd

LDA, Findel Education, 2 Gregory Street, Hyde, Cheshire SK14 4HR

www.ldalearning.com

The right of Lois M. Addy to be identified as the author of this work has been asserted in accordance with Sections 77 and 78 of the Copyright, Designs and Patents Act 1988.

CONTENTS

ABBREVIATIONS

ADHD	attention deficit (hyperactivity) disorder
AP	alternative provision
AWPU	age-weighted pupil unit
BESD	behaviour, emotional and social difficulties
CAMHS	Child and Adolescent Mental Health Services
CCG	clinical commissioning group
CDC	Council for Disabled Children
CEA	continuity of education allowance
CEAS	Children's Education Advisory Service
CoP	Code of Practice
CPD	continuing professional development
DCD	developmental co-ordination disorder (formerly dyspraxia)
DES	Department of Education and Science (1964–92)
DfBIS	Department for Business, Innovation and Skills
DfCSF	Department for Children, Schools and Families (2007–10)
DfE	Department for Education (1992–95, 2010–)
DfEE	Department for Education and Employment (1995–2001)
DfES	Department for Education and Skills (2001–07)
DISS	Deployment and Impact of Support Staff
DH	Department of Health
DHO	designated health officer
DT	designated teacher
EHC	education, health and care
ESN(M)	educationally subnormal (moderate)
ESN(S)	educationally subnormal (severe)
EHCAR	education, health and care assessment request
EY	early years
EYFS	early years foundation stage
EYFSP	early years foundation stage profile
EYP	early years practitioner
FE	further education
FSM	free school meals
HE	higher education

HLTA	higher level teaching assistant
IAR	individually assigned resources
IAS	informal advice and support
ICF	International Classification of Function, Disability and Health
INMSS	independent and non-maintained special schools
inset	in service training
IS	independent supporter
ISF	individual service fund
ISP	independent specialist provider
LA	local authority
LDA	learning difficulty assessment
LDD	learning difficulties or disabilities
LO	local offer
MLD	moderate learning difficulties
MOD	Ministry of Defence
NAHT	National Association of Head Teachers
Ofsted	Office for Standards in Education, Children's Services and Skills
PCT	primary care trust
PEP	personal education plan
PfA	Preparing for Adulthood
PP	pathway plan
PPS	parent partnership service
PRU	pupil referral unit
QTS	qualified teacher status
SA	School Action
SA+	School Action Plus
SALT	speech and language therapist/therapy
SEN	special educational needs
SENA	special educational needs addition
SENCo	special educational needs co-ordinator
SEND	special educational needs and/or disability
SENDA	Special Educational Needs and Disability Act (2001)
SENDIST	Special Educational Needs and Disability Tribunal
SENAP	Special Educational Needs Assessment Panel
SLD	severe learning difficulties
SMEH	social, mental and emotional health
SpLD	specific learning difficulties
TA	teaching assistant
TAC	team-around-the-child
WHO	World Health Organization
VSH	virtual school head

PREFACE

The Government has recently concluded its most comprehensive revalidation of special educational needs for over 30 years. The aim of this book is to simplify and draw together the plethora of new legislation, policy and guidance to help all those who support pupils with special educational needs and/or disability. It provides practical examples and case studies to guide busy practitioners in completing relevant documentation. It also include quizzes, photocopiable information and activities that can be used to explain the legislation to others. Most chapters conclude with a summary of implications for members of the school or setting leadership team, SENCos, teachers and governors.

Please note that while every effort has been made to use inclusive language, 'child' has been used to refer to children from birth to 16 years, and 'young person' from ages 16 to 25 years. The term 'parent' has been used for the sake of brevity in many cases, but can also refer to carers of children and young people.

CHAPTER 1
How far have we come?

The education of pupils with learning differences has been long and eventful, culminating in the radical reforms of 2014. The journey to our current position shows how far we have come to make the inclusion and acceptance of *all* children a reality. It also reminds us why we may continue to be apprehensive when new procedures are put in place.

We start our journey in the 1800s, at a time when there was a marked distinction between the rich and the underprivileged. The majority were poor and lived in crowded, unsanitary spaces, often without a bed to sleep on; smoke from chimneys made it a dirty environment to bring up children and infant mortality was very high with only about 140 babies out of 1000 live births surviving their first year of life. These conditions exposed the population to epidemics such as smallpox, cholera, tuberculosis and polio, resulting in disability, disfigurement and death.

The Industrial Revolution heralded further hardship as people moved from rural to urban areas in pursuit of employment and meagre wages, resulting in increasing overpopulation in towns and cities. Children as young as six worked for up to 14 hours for a pittance in dangerous and unprotected environments with little regard for their health and safety. At this time children with a disability or illness had very little chance of survival.

Those 'delicate' children from more affluent backgrounds were 'cared for' by their families or 'nursed' by governesses; segregated from their peers in all aspects of education. Those with severe learning difficulties were confined to same-sex mental handicap or disability institutions (lunatic asylums) usually located on the periphery of cities and towns.

At this time children with less overt needs were assessed in reading and writing and, as part of the teacher's salary depended on the pass rate, many children were expelled from school and were unable to continue their education. This rejection of 'slow learning and emotionally disturbed' children led to the expansion of the special school sector established by philanthropists such as Barnardo and Lord Shaftesbury. Lord Shaftesbury formed the Ragged School Union in 1844 and by 1852 there were over 200 free schools for poor children in Britain (Frederickson & Cline, 2009).

Special schools were also established to 'care' for children, and provide basic literacy and numeracy skills where appropriate. However, this setting meant that those with a physical and/or learning difficulty were denied the day-to-day experience of living and growing up with their non-disabled peers and siblings. It also meant that those with learning needs and/or a physical disability had no voice, no rights and no expectations!

Changes started to occur in the 1920s in the aftermath of the First World War. The 'heroes of our country' returned home with extensive physical injuries, head injuries resulting in learning difficulties and trauma-induced mental illness. They found little support available to them, they had no legal rights and few job prospects. These veterans, together with those born with a disability, formed the first disability movement and collectively lobbied the Government against discrimination. As a result, the Government introduced in a 3% quota system which forced employers to take on registered disabled employees.

The Second World War added momentum to this movement and started to change people's perceptions of disability, whether this ranged from those injured during the war to children and young people with a learning and/or physical disability.

In 1943 the Norwood Report was commissioned to review the education of children with learning differences and disabilities. This report suggested that at 11 years old children with learning differences *could* contribute to society; however, they would need to focus on attaining academic, technical or manual skills to achieve a level of productivity. At this time children with severe learning difficulties were known as 'educationally subnormal – moderate' (ESN(M)) or 'educationally subnormal – severe' (ESN(S)) depending on the extent of the difficulty. Some were 'educated' in special schools, others were not considered capable of benefitting from education; instead they were provided with training centres run by health professionals. These recommendations became legislation through the Education Act 1944.

A further legacy of the Second World War was the desire to introduce a comprehensive health and welfare service which would be free to all. This led to the guidance in the form of the National Health Service Act 1946, and the subsequent establishment of the National Health Service (NHS) in England and Wales, and separately in Scotland in 1947. The National Assistance Act (1948) replaced the Poor Law (1930) to see the start of a welfare state, and with it the beginning of the end of the 'worthy poor' charitable approach to those with a disability or learning difference. Despite this shift in thinking, language originating from this philanthropic period remains today: expressions such as 'What a pity!' and 'What a shame!' are still evident and reflect societal perspectives of learning and physical disability. These terms have their origin in 'those to be pitied' and 'those of whom one is ashamed'!

In the 1950s and 60s the disability movement for children and young people gained further momentum in the growth of the charitable sectors. In 1952 the Spastic Society (now Scope) was founded by three parents and a social worker who wanted children with a disability, particularly those with cerebral palsy, to have equal rights to an education.

By the mid 1960s, with the burgeoning post-war economic recovery, there was a positive move towards 'normalisation'; embracing differences and individuality. In 1968 Dunn suggested that there was little evidence to show that children with special needs educated in special schools did any better than those educated in mainstream schools. This led to the introduction of the Education (Handicapped Children) Act 1970 which removed the distinction between those who were and were not educable in school, and led to a more integrated attitude towards educating children with special needs and/or a physical disability (SEND).

In 1978, Mary Warnock, an influential figure in education, took this further by highlighting the fact that many children with SEND still had to travel unreasonable distances to attend those schools who were willing to accept them, thereby reinforcing a segregated approach. The Warnock Report recommended that a continuum of services be established to support locational, social and functional integration (Warnock, 1978).

Warnock felt that children should be physically able to access their local school, interact and learn with children who did not have overt differences and jointly participate in educational programmes. Her committee also recommended that the derogatory terms ESN(M) and ESN(S) be replaced with 'moderate learning difficulties' (MLD) and 'severe learning difficulties' (SLD).

Warnock's recommendations led to the implementation of the Education Act 1981, which shifted the focus from separate or alternative provision to provision within mainstream schools. The intention was to shift the attention away from the child's innate disability and instead focus on their difficulties related to learning. However, pupils were still expected to fit into an established education system, rather than the system adapting to accommodate and include the individual.

The cardinal, decisive step towards further integration was the formulation of the National Curriculum (1988) and the Department of Education and Science's declaration that **each pupil** should have a broad and balanced curriculum

Mary Warnock © 2010 Ian Tovey, reproduced by permission of *The Spectator*

differentiated by their particular needs (DfES, 1989). Unfortunately, some schools still rejected children on the basis that they did not have the expertise to meet certain pupils' 'particular needs'.

The Education Act 1996 was introduced to stop this, placing a duty on schools to include all children with SEND in a mainstream school, so long as:

- O the child's needs were properly met
- O other children's education was not adversely affected
- O resources were being used efficiently
- O parents were in agreement with the placement.

Prejudices still abounded both in the classroom and in the playground and the excuse that 'other children's learning would be adversely affected' if a pupil with an overt need were to be accepted into the school was often used as a reason to prevent admission.

The Special Educational Needs and Disability Act (SENDA) 2001 challenged this practice by bringing together the Disability Discrimination Act 1995 and special needs legislation, making it unlawful to discriminate against disabled pupils in any aspect of school life. A Special Educational Needs and Disability Tribunal (SENDIST) was established to challenge any case of discrimination.

Accompanying SENDA 2001 was a Code of Practice (CoP) (Department for Education and Skills, 2001) to implement the procedures set out in the Act. This included a stepped approach to addressing pupil need.

A square peg in a round hole?

The terms School Action (SA) and School Action Plus (SA+) were coined to indicate the complexity of need and level of support required. Pupils with very complex needs were required to have a **statutory assessment**. This was a detailed assessment of need and involved the collation of information from multiple sources including health and social care. The assessment concluded with a **statement of needs** which indicated the precise support which was needed to help the pupil access the curriculum. This was referred to as the **statementing** procedure. This indicated a range of support required and more often than not included the provision of a non-teaching assistant. The statement often focused on the hours of personal support needed, rather than the range of adjustments which would enable the pupil to learn effectively.

The SENDA and its outworking in the CoP 2001 stipulated:

- a stronger right for children with SEND to be educated within a mainstream school
- a new requirement for schools and relevant nursery education providers to tell parents when they were making special educational provision for their child
- a new right for schools and relevant nursery education providers to request a **statutory assessment** of a child's learning needs
- a remit of 26 weeks to complete the legal process for identifying and assessing special needs and, where appropriate, issue a legally binding statement on how those needs would be met
- separate directives on early years, primary and secondary phases
- guidance on working in partnership with parents
- pupil participation in determining their learning needs
- working in partnership with other agencies, (i.e. health and social care)
- a stepped approach to identifying need, establishing the categories of SA and SA+, before applying for a statutory assessment of a child's learning needs
- Ofsted inspectors' involvement in evaluating SEND policies and practices
- that schools draw up, publish and report on their SEND policy.

This legislation was not changed until 2011 when it was felt that a **radical review** of SEND education was required.

Implications for the leadership team

- Setting leaders need to ensure that inclusive principles should apply to all aspects of the curriculum and should not be an adjunct to mainstream practice.
- Setting leaders need to make sure that the terminology used is inclusive and politically correct.
- Educational practice should value the uniqueness of every individual.
- There should be no place for prejudice in any facet of teaching or setting.

Implications for SENCos

● SENCos need to exemplify inclusive practice by using appropriate terminology, referring to the individual before their disability. For example, referring to the individual as a person with CP (cerebral palsy), rather than 'a CP'.

● SENCos needs to be aware that prejudice still exists, with some parents believing that their child's education is affected by the presence of those with SEND. Strategies need to be put into place to alleviate these fears and to perpetuate a positive spirit of acceptance among pupils and parents alike.

Implications for teachers

● Input regarding SEND may have been lacking in the teacher training years, therefore teachers may need to make a considerable commitment and effort to understand pupils with a wide range of physical and learning needs.

● Teachers must be challenged to embrace inclusion in its entirety, considering the differences between the paradigms of segregation, integration and inclusion.

Implications for governors

● Governors need to have a good understanding of the legislative drivers which have led to the current educational reforms.

● Governors are in an excellent position to dispel parental concerns regarding the amount of time spent on pupils with SEND and to debate positive strategies to alleviate disruption to the learning of other children.

CHAPTER 2
What triggered the review of SEND education?

In July 2005, Baroness Warnock wrote an article on SEND in which she called for the Government to set up an **urgent** commission to review the SEND situation (Warnock, 2005). She was particularly concerned that the concept of inclusion had lost its way, the process of 'statementing' had developed into a resource allocation plan, and that the link between social disadvantage and SEND had not been addressed and indeed had widened. She felt that the concept of the 'statement of need' had become overused, as parents began to believe that without a statement their child or young person would get no extra help. A battle between parents and local authorities (LAs) had commenced. The original intent was that only 2% of the population would have needs so complex that they warranted a 'statement'. The reality was that over 20% requested this extensive assessment.

Baroness Warnock also became increasingly concerned by the lack of support that was being offered to those whose difficulties were less overt. She referred to these as the 'hidden handicap' of specific learning difficulties (SpLD) such as dyslexia, dyscalculia and developmental co-ordination disorder (DCD). She was also troubled that academically able pupils who found the social aspects of education a challenge, such as those with Asperger's syndrome, were being failed by the current system. To summarise her concerns:

> *I think to suppose that because a child is under the same roof as all his peers he is therefore included, that is a terrible delusion.*
> Warnock, 2008

- O Inclusion was **not** working and a new commission was needed to look into the whole area of SEND provision.

- O Too many statements were being requested because parents and teachers believed that additional support and resources were necessary and that these could only be available on completion of this statement.

- O Small specialist schools had a role in supporting pupils with more complex needs, especially those on the autistic spectrum, and their role needed to be acknowledged.

- O Bullying of children with SEND had become an inevitable part of mainstream school.

- O SEND should only be catered for in mainstream schools when needs could be met from within the school's own resources.

Particular concerns focused on the use of statements:

○ Statements had served their time and had been overused.

○ The concept of a statement, and the criteria for deciding who should have a statement, had never been clear.

○ Pupils with similar needs were getting entirely different provision, depending on the availability, and distribution of, LA funding. This was causing a postcode lottery.

○ Statements had become overtly linked to available resources, not to the pupil's needs.

○ Some statements were written based on what the LA could afford.

○ There was a mismatch between what the statement said and what was provided, depending on resources and staffing availability.

○ There was a danger that the system benefitted the most eloquent parents, who were able to manipulate the system to obtain services for their child.

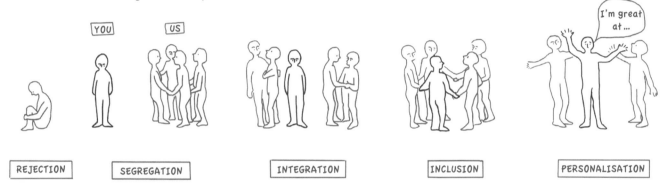

From rejection and exclusion to inclusion and personalisation

Baroness Warnock's concerns were reinforced in 2009, when Brian Lamb was commissioned to evaluate parental confidence in the SEND assessment system. He found that while some parents reported a positive experience of the assessment process, others had encountered endless problems based on poor communication between home and school, limitations in teacher knowledge of SEND and lowered expectations for their child or young person.

Lamb identified the following concerns:

○ There were limitations in the systematic monitoring of schools' performance in SEND.

○ Parents were passed from pillar to post and needed to battle bureaucracy and frustration as they sought to gain the information they needed to support their child.

○ Children were repeatedly assessed by different agencies, who were often seeking the same information.

○ There were several shortfalls in support from colleagues working in health and social services, particularly therapies such as Child and Adolescent Mental Health Services (CAMHS).

○ Pupils with SEND were not achieving their potential. By the time they left school they were more than twice as likely to be out of education, training or employment as those without SEND (DfE, 2011a).

According to the Council for Disabled Children, on average, a child with a disability experiences over 32 assessments during their childhood years.

○ Life chances for the approximately two million children and young people in England who were identified as having a SEND were disproportionately poor (DfE, 2009).

○ Children and young people with SEND said that they felt frustrated by a lack of the **right** help at school or from other services.

○ Families had to put up with a culture of low expectations.

He summarised these concerns into four recommendations for revising the SEND system:

1 Children's outcomes needed to be at the heart of the system.

2 Parents should have a stronger voice.

3 The system should have a greater focus on the needs of children and young people, rather than on indicative labels.

4 The system needed to be more accountable in order to deliver better services.

> *Much current integration practice was in fact the sharing of communal space or an activity, with the non-disabled, but not necessarily on an equal footing.*
> Mackey & McQueen, 1998

The concerns of Mary Warnock and Brian Lamb were supported by other influential reviews. These included:

Better communication: A review of services for children and young people 0–19 with speech, language and communication needs by John Bercow (DCSF, 2008).

Identifying and teaching children and young people with dyslexia and literacy difficulties led by Sir Jim Rose, (DCSF, 2009b).

The Salt Review: Independent review of teacher supply for pupils with severe, profound and multiple learning difficulties led by Toby Salt (DCSF, 2010).

The special educational needs and disability review: A statement is not enough (Ofsted, 2010).

Progression post-16 for learners with learning difficulties and/or disabilities (Ofsted, 2011).

Adult social care (Law Commission, 2011).

In 2012/13, the Local Government Ombudsman received more complaints about education and children's services than any other area. From 20,186 complaints, 8.6% related to SEN provision.

Some of the most significant areas of concern were:

- delays in the process, leading to other problems, such as the loss of education
- inadequate assessment and review of statements of SEND
- poor planning of an individual's SEND support, particularly in the key transition phases
- failure to provide specific SEND support, such as qualified specialists
- wrongful exclusion of children from the educational system due to their SEND
- failure to ensure suitable SEND provision in a council's area.

Local Government Ombudsman, 2014

During this period the Equality Act 2010 was published. This strengthened the inclusion movement by quashing subtle potentially discriminatory practices based on perception, prejudice and ignorance.

New proposals were suggested and collated into the Green Paper: Support and aspiration: A new approach to special educational needs and disability (DfE, 2011a). An extensive consultation period began, resulting in the current legislation and guidance.

The detail of this guidance is examined in the chapters that follow.

Quiz: How far have we come?

Match the event on the left with the correct date on the right.

Equality Act	1988
Removing Barriers to Achievement	1970
Mental Deficiency Act	2003
Warnock Report	1907
National Curriculum	2001
Disability Discrimination Act	2014
Rose Review of Literacy	2011
Special Educational Needs and Disability Act (SENDA)	1978
Education (Handicapped) Act	2010
Eugenics Education Society	2009
Education Act (following the Norwood Report)	2004
Children and Families Act	1913
Every Child Matters	1995
Support and aspiration: a new approach to SEND	1944
Lamb Enquiry	2006

Answers are on page 96.

Implications for the leadership team

● Leaders need to learn from the mistakes made in SEND provision in the past, as highlighted by the commissioned work of Warnock, Lamb, Bercow, Rose and Salt.

● Recommendations highlighted in these reviews should inform curriculum planning, particularly in relation to pupils with SEND.

● Leaders need to conduct a critical analysis of SEND provision to review the outcomes and achievements of pupils with SEND.

Implications for SENCos

● SENCos will need a full understanding of the rationale for change and therefore need to be familiar with the reports and recommendations which have led to current SEND reform.

● SENCos need to be aware of how the original provision for those with SEN has been distorted and eroded, leading to a dependency on statements for meeting pupil need.

Implications for teachers

● Teachers need to be aware of the criticisms regarding the outcomes for pupils with SEND, and the rationale for change.

● Teachers will need to reflect on the teaching strategies that they have previously adopted for pupils with SEND and consider whether their aspirations were high enough and whether the pupils have achieved their learning potential.

Implications for governors

● Governors need to spend time with the school leadership team, reflecting on the concerns raised by Warnock and Lamb and considering to what extent they may apply to the school's policy and practice.

● Governors need to ensure that the school's vision promotes the inclusion of all pupils with SEND.

● Governors would be wise to obtain information regarding the personal experience of current and former pupils with SEND and their families prior to the implementation of the new reforms.

CHAPTER 3
Equality Act 2010

The Equality Act 2010 was introduced to draw together all anti-discriminatory law in relation to race, gender, sexuality and disability. This combined a massive nine Acts of Parliament and over 100 regulations! One key section of this Act is dedicated to the rights of children with SEND. This makes it unlawful for any school, whether classified as a special school, academy, independent or free school, to discriminate on the grounds of disability, race, sex, gender reassignment, religion or belief.

The Act stipulates that admission arrangements to nurseries, schools and colleges must be reasonable, and that a child with a disability or learning need must not be unfairly disadvantaged by the admission criteria (either directly or indirectly). Therefore, for example, the refusal to admit a child to a setting on the basis that the school layout cannot accommodate a child in a wheelchair is not acceptable, unless the setting absolutely cannot be adapted at all, i.e. is a listed building.

The Act requires schools to make **reasonable adjustments** to support pupils with extra needs so that they are able to join in as many school activities as possible. This includes going on school trips and participating in school-based clubs. The Act stresses the need to pre-empt a child's needs so that there is no conflict or dispute when the need arises. For example, if a trip is planned to a local zoo, school staff must consider what sort of transport and support is required to include a child with quadriplegic cerebral palsy, who may be wheelchair dependent. Similarly, if a trip was planned to the theatre, what support would be available to a child with autism who was frightened of loud bangs and flashing lights?

The term **reasonable adjustment** is a loose term and can mean different things to different people. The crux of this matter is the school's duty to avoid placing the child at a 'substantial disadvantage'; 'substantial' being defined as anything more than a minor or trivial disadvantage. The following questions can help determine whether the adjustment is possible:

- Is it effective, will it help the child or young person to participate or learn?
- Is it practical?
- What are the costs?
- Are resources available?
- Is there any financial support available for the adjustment?
- Have any changes already been made?
- Is the cost prohibitive for the size of the school or setting?

○ Is there a health and safety risk to the child, other pupils or support staff?

○ Will standards be maintained, academic or otherwise?

It may also be pertinent to ask:

○ Would other children benefit from the accommodations?

○ Would it protect all vulnerable children?

○ Will it relieve the concerns of parents?

Here are a few examples of the types of adjustment that could be made:

Physical accommodations	Personal assistance
Alteration of steps and stairs (provision of ramps or lifts)	Language interpreters
Levelling or widening of passageways and paths	Support staff
Widening of entrances and exits	Nursing care
Adapting internal and external doors for ease of access, such as installing sliding or bifold doors or electronic opening devices	British Sign Language interpreters
Making toilets accessible	Readers
Improving the clarity of signs	Moving and lifting personnel
Altering lighting and ventilation	Teaching assistants
Reducing classroom clutter	Volunteers to support school trips

Auxiliary aids	Educational practices
Coloured overlays for pupils with dyslexia	Flexibility in timetabling
Adapted PE equipment	Allowing time to attend medical clinics or therapy sessions
Adapted keyboards	Differentiating teaching materials
Electronic or manual note-taking services	Changing font on printed hand-outs
Induction loop or infrared broadcast system	Providing information in alternative formats, such as Braille or audio CDs
Audio-visual fire alarms	Modifying procedures for testing or assessment
Privacy boards	Changing classroom seating plans to optimise attention
Ear defenders	
Writing boards	
Weighted lap blankets	
Ball seats	
Quiet space tents	
Ergonomic writing tools	
Computer software	

The Equality Act prevents the following:

○ **Direct discrimination.** This is when a pupil is treated less favourably than another pupil because of their disability or learning difficulty, i.e. deliberately avoiding asking a pupil with a speech impediment to contribute to a whole-class discussion. This behaviour suggests that the pupil is being discriminated against due to the **perception** that he/she might be unable to cope. This might be based on a previous difficult experience or an **assumption** that the pupil would not want to participate for fear of being ridiculed by classmates.

Case study

I work in supporting a little boy who has autism in school. Today he went over to the art table and seemed to be taking an interest (I was excited to see this because it is usually a nightmare to get him to do anything art-related at school). The temporary teacher who was running the art table grabbed his hand away from it and said to me, 'He can't do this. He doesn't have the capacity to understand how to do it and he'll get glue all over the place.' (The activity was papier-mâché.)

Was this temporary teacher discriminatory?

○ **Indirect discrimination.** This can occur if no accommodations are put into place to help an individual learn. For example, a teacher might believe that it is more inclusive to give all pupils the same work. A 'see how they get on' mentality may be in place. But the lack of support may highlight the individual's difficulties, causing them embarrassment and resulting in low self-confidence and self-esteem. If this approach cannot be justified or does not have a legitimate aim, it is indirect discrimination.

○ **Discrimination arising from disability.** This occurs when a pupil with a disability is treated unfavourably because of something related to their disability. For example, a pupil might not be allowed to participate in a PE lesson due to the nature of the lesson and/or the fear that their wheelchair could be an obstruction to others.

○ **Failure to make reasonable adjustments.** This was referred to earlier in the chapter and is the most subtle form of discrimination. The Act can be used to help pupils in many aspects of the curriculum, including access assessments and examinations. This requires an awarding body to make reasonable adjustments which may be unique to the individual pupil and may not be included in the list of available access arrangements. However, there is no duty on the awarding body to make any adjustment to the assessment objectives being tested.

The Equality Act 2010 also refers to the harassment and victimisation of pupils:

○ **Harassment** is defined as having the purpose or effect of violating a pupil's dignity or creating an intimidating, hostile, degrading, humiliating or offensive environment for the pupil. This might include a teacher constantly shouting at a pupil who has difficulties with attention and concentration due to a developmental difficulty.

The term of harassment could also be applied to a teacher who shouted at a pupil for failing to carry out an instruction in a prompt manner: a pupil with receptive language difficulties may have either misunderstood what was being asked or needed more time to process the instruction.

Case study

A boy with muscular dystrophy felt that he was being harassed by his form tutor, who constantly asked him whether he was feeling alright, even though his parents had asked him not to do this in front of the other boys.

Even though the teacher thought he was being kind and had no intention of hurting or humiliating him, this could still count as harassment if the boy found it distressing.

I remember how much I got bullied in school and the trouble I would get into. The teachers and principal said I was the centre of the disruptions never mind the fact I never initiated them and mostly got trounced rather badly. Having Asperger's syndrome and picked on in school go hand in hand I suppose!

Online forum

O **Sexual harassment** is also highlighted under the Act, this being unwanted behaviour of a sexual nature which has the purpose or effect of violating a pupil's dignity, or creating an intimidating and hostile, degrading, humiliating or offensive environment for the pupil. Unfortunately this is not as uncommon as presumed. There is considerable evidence that children with learning difficulties are three to four times more likely to be abused than their able-bodied peers.

There are several reasons for this, some relating back to the prejudices and attitudes highlighted in Chapter 1. Children who have limited communication skills and/or a physical disability may be unable to physically withdraw quickly from a potentially threatening situation, leaving them susceptible to abuse or assault (Sullivan & Knutson, 2000).

O A further concern is treating pupils less favourably because they reject harassment related to sex.

The Act also prohibits **victimisation**. This is defined as treating a pupil badly because they or their parent or sibling intends to:

O make a claim or complaint of discrimination under the Act

O give evidence or information to support another person's claim under the Act

O allege that the school or someone else has breached the Act.

One of the unique features of the Act is that **positive discrimination** is allowed for pupils with SEND. There are occasions when it is acceptable to treat a child/young person with a disability or SEN more favourably because of their disability. For example, a school may provide extra lessons to a pupil who has missed them due to medical appointments relating to their disability.

Enforcement

An appreciation of the Equality Act 2010 is essential for all educators. If equality measures are not implemented effectively the consequences are serious, as the overall Ofsted inspection grade for the establishment may be affected, even if all other aspects of the school are outstanding.

It is possible for individual pupils to bring proceedings against their school in the county courts for alleged contraventions of the equality provisions. In addition, county courts have the power to award declarations, injunctions and damages to the pupil. The Equality and Human Rights Commission can also take its own independent action against schools if it suspects that it is committing an unlawful act and it can serve its own notices on the school or apply to the courts for further action to be taken. Breaches of the equality provisions can therefore have significant consequences for schools.

Quiz: Equality Act 2010 (1)

Answer the following questions to test your knowledge.

1	**When was the Equality Act introduced in Britain?**
	a 1972
	b 1997
	c 2010
2	**How many protected characteristics are there?**
	a 6
	b 9
	c 12
3	**Which part of the Act addresses pupils with special educational needs?**
	a Part 2
	b Part 6
	c Part 7
4	**What are the areas of unlawful discrimination known as?**
	a Equality strands
	b Diversity dimensions
	c Protected characteristics
	d Unfairness grounds
5	**What strand of equality is not covered by the Equality Act 2010?**
	a Age
	b Gender
	c Economic background
6	**Name one specific duty all schools must meet.**
	a Publish a policy statement
	b Have due regard for certain needs
	c Treat all people the same
	d Collect equality data on all staff
7	**What are reasonable adjustments?**
	a Actions which prevent disabled pupils being placed at a substantial disadvantage compared to their peers.
	b Informing the class that the pupil has some difficulties which require their help.
	c Actions suggested by the pupil to enable them to learn more effectively.
8	**The prevalence and profile of disability varies by ethnicity.**
	True / False
9	**What percentage of the English population have a special need?**
	a 10%
	b 29%
	c 18%

Quiz: Equality Act 2010 (2)

10	What word describes the less favourable treatment of someone because they have made a complaint in relation to the treatment that they have received as a result of bullying or harassment? **a** Toleration **b** Victimisation **c** Ignoring
11	A disability has to be permanent to be recognised. True / False
12	To which organisations does the vast majority of the Equality Act apply? **a** Public sector **b** Private sector **c** Voluntary and community sector **d** All
13	What does it mean when they say that 'the duty is anticipatory'? **a** Teachers only need to act when a problem/issue is raised. **b** The school should anticipate the child's requirements. **c** Children should anticipate their difficulties and let staff know how they should respond.
14	An independent fee-paying school provides a child who stammers with some one-to-one support from an adult, as required by its reasonable adjustment duty to provide auxiliary services. Can the school charge extra for this? Yes / No
15	The Equality Act extends the reasonable adjustment duty to require schools to provide auxiliary aids and services to disabled pupils. True / False
16	The Equality Act allows school staff to treat disabled pupils more favourably than non-disabled pupils. True / False

Answers are on page 96.

Implications for the leadership team

🛈 Leaders of every setting must be aware of their duty not to discriminate against children or pupils (including prospective and former pupils) in relation to:
- its admissions procedures
- exclusions
- the provision of education
- access to any benefits, facilities or services.

🛈 Leaders must take a proactive approach to promoting disability equality and eliminating discrimination. This means that setting leaders will need to think about how their buildings, routines and practices impact on **everyone**!

🛈 Leaders must ensure there is clear effective policy and practice on behaviour and language.

🛈 In school settings, leaders are still required to have accessibility plans. These must show how the school:
- can enable the pupil with SEND to participate in the curriculum
- has improved the physical environment to enable those with disabilities to take better advantage of the education, benefits, facilities and services provided
- has improved the availability and accessibility of information to those with disabilities.

🛈 From an employment perspective, it is now unlawful for setting leaders to ask health-related questions of applicants for care, teaching and non-teaching posts, unless the questions are specifically related to an intrinsic function of the work. This means that setting leaders cannot ask job applicants to complete a generic health questionnaire as part of the application procedure.

Implications for SENCos

🛈 SENCos will need to obtain objective information regarding the pupil's experience of school, their education and access to the curriculum. This can be obtained using:
- pupil voice questionnaires
- online questionnaires (using Google Survey, Formic, Survey Monkey etc.)
- talking mats (one-to-one interviews)
- parent/carer annual focus groups.

🛈 SENCos must prepare information for pupils, parents and the community that is accessible to them. This might mean using different formats, such as Widgit symbols or Braille, using a larger or different font, summarising information or simplifying the language used.

🛈 SENCos may also need to put arrangements in place to help parents with a disability to attend a school event, such as a parents' evening or school performance. For example, a wheelchair-accessible room may be necessary for a parent with reduced mobility.

Implications for teachers

- Teachers must put aside any negative views about SEND and ensure that, whenever possible, they have considered how to fully engage the pupil with SEND in every lesson. This may involve adapting materials so they can be manipulated and/or allowing pupils to present their written work in a different way.

- Teachers must be able to explain to parents how the curriculum is differentiated to enable their child with SEND to fully participate.

- Teachers should ensure that the diversity of the population, including disability, is represented in teaching material.

Implications for governors

- Governors must ensure that school policies reflect Equality duties.

- For the most part, the school's legal duties remain the same; however, schools must now provide auxiliary aids and services to pupils with SEND.

- Governors need to appreciate that accommodations should be provided on a needs-based approach and cannot work on a one-size-fits-all approach.

CHAPTER 4
Children and Families Act 2014

The Children and Families Act received Royal assent on 13 March 2014 and provided clear directives in the following areas:

- adoption
- family justice
- child welfare
- the role of the Children's Commissioner for England
- children and young people with SEN and disabilities
- childcare
- parents' rights.

Part 3 of the Act focuses on the needs of children and young people with SEN and disabilities and was actioned in the new SEN Code of Practice (CoP) in September 2014 (DfE & DH, 2014).

Here is a summary of the key changes highlighted in this legislation for pupils with SEN:

Previously	Now
Special Educational Needs and Disability Act 2001 and CoP 2001	Children and Families Act 2014 implemented through the SEN CoP 2014
Reliance on 'diagnosis' leading to lowered expectations	Focus on learning need, establishing aspirational targets
Categories of need: • School Action (SA) • School Action Plus (SA+)	Removal of these categories and emphasis on a 'graduated approach' to supporting pupils with SEN
Statutory assessment of SEN	Introduction of education, health and care (EHC) plans
Recommendations by health and social care professionals not legally binding	Health and social care contribution to EHC plans and implementation through joint commissioning of services
Assessment by many different professionals	Collaborative assessment

Previously	Now
SEN budget controlled by local authority (LA) and allocated according to a very complicated funding formula	Schools have control of notional SEN budget, based on simplified formulae with top-up budget (controlled by the LA) available for pupils with complex needs
No option for personal budget	Option of a personal budget (for some pupils, not all)
Information about support available to pupils and parents of children and young people with SEN must be found from multiple sources	Requirement to publish a central local offer (LO) of support available from all agencies within the LA, including charities and support groups
Encouragement to involve pupils and families in decision-making process	Explicit requirements to involve pupils and parents in SEN provision
Remit: children and young people from 2–18 years	Remit: children and young people from 0–25 years
Young people over 16 described as having 'learning difficulties and disabilities'	Young people over 16 now referred to as having 'special educational needs'

The practical outworking of the legislation relating to children and young people with SEN is explained in detail in the CoP 2014. The implications for educators will be described in the following chapters.

CHAPTER 5
Principles of the SEN Code of Practice 2014

The practical outworking of the legislation relating to children and young people with SEN contained in the Equality Act 2010 and the Children and Families Act 2014 is explained in detail in the SEN Code of Practice (CoP) 2014 which became law in September 2014, although a period of three years has been allowed for the development and transfer of certain processes, such as the transfer of statements into education, health and care (EHC) plans.

The guidance applies to all mainstream and special schools, academies (in all their forms including free schools and studio schools) and further education (FE) institutions. The CoP begins by defining SEN as continuing to refer to those who have:

- a greater difficulty in learning than the majority of other children
- a disability which prevents or hinders them from making use of the educational facilities generally provided in the area.

This definition applies to pre-school children also.

The main change in terminology refers to young people over 16 who were previously described as having 'learning difficulties and disabilities'. Under the new CoP they will be regarded as having SEN in the same way as if they were under 16.

The first chapter of the CoP places the child or young person securely at the centre of every aspect of service delivery and planning, and while this may, for many, be commonplace, for some the reality has differed enormously. Difficult decisions regarding the allocation of a finite budget has led to many services being cost-led: based on what can be afforded, rather than what the child or young person actually needs. The Children and Families Act 2014 provides the legislative strength to turn the rhetoric of person-centred practice into a reality.

Previously services were established and parents and carers, children and young people were asked their opinion of them. The new CoP turns this around by encouraging educators and service providers to ask:

- What do you need?
- What would you like to achieve?
- How can we help you?
- What are your aspirations?
- What can we do to help you realise your goals?

This approach is being used to rethink many services. For example, parents and carers, young adults and children are now expected to be involved in developing the content of the local offer (LO). This provides clear guidance on the services available to meet the needs of those with SEN in a local authority (LA). In all settings, staff must take into account parent/carer preferences when applying for, and participating in, pre-school nurseries, schools or further or higher education (FE/HE) establishments. Schools must highlight the individual's aspirations when establishing education objectives, and any EHC plan must reflect the individual's own aspirations and hopes f or the future.

The emphasis is on person-centred planning involving pupil and parent. This may require creativity and flexibility in order to acknowledge the wishes of parents or carers who may themselves have learning difficulties, a sensory or physical impairment, cultural differences, or whose first language is not English. The resulting published plan must reflect these differences.

The CoP echoes the need for inclusive practice and the removal of barriers to learning expressed in the Equality Act 2010 and the Children and Families Act 2014. Educators are discouraged from identifying children and young people with learning difficulties too quickly, and are instead encouraged to view all children as having learning needs that warrant Quality First Teaching. The removal of the terms School Action and School Action Plus reinforce this, with the intention that only those pupils with highly complex needs will require an EHC plan and high needs funding. The remaining pupils are expected to have their needs met using the school's own resources.

By labelling so many children as 'special needs', we betray those who really do need help.

Stevens, 2012

Less emphasis is now being placed on the identification of SEN and labelling of the learning difficulty, preferring instead to refer to the pupil's functional or learning need. Section 1.24 of the CoP encourages teachers to provide 'high quality teaching that is differentiated and personalised, that will meet the individual needs of the majority of children and young people, and pupils with additional learning needs.'

Inclusion requires striving for the optimal growth of all pupils in the most enabling environment by recognising individual strengths and needs.

Council for Disabled Children, 2008

There is a strong view that it will increasingly be those children and young people with an EHC plan and highly complex needs that will be able to access special schooling. Section 1.27 of the CoP states that 'where a child or young person has SEN but does not have an EHC plan **they must be educated in a mainstream setting** except in specific circumstances.'

The further emphasis is on ensuring that any intervention is based on the **best available evidence**, with **clearly measurable outcomes**. This requires the teacher to become a scientific practitioner and critically analyse the interventions they are using from the perspective of its research base. Often, interventions are judged by the difference they make to a pupil's learning with a focus on levels of improvement and ratio gains. The CoP has extended this by encouraging teachers to be more cognisant of the origins, development and parameters of interventions so that teaching becomes more clearly focused and cost effective. This approach may be new to many teachers, and therefore further training may be required to ensure that evidence-informed practice permeates the curriculum.

I think there is a huge prize waiting to be claimed by teachers. By collecting better evidence about what works best, and establishing a culture where this evidence is used as a matter of routine, we can improve outcomes for children, and increase professional independence.

Goldacre, 2013

Implications for the leadership team

- School leaders in mainstream schools must plan for educating an increasing number of children and young people with a wide range of complex learning needs. Approximately 18.7% of children and young people in England have a SEN (DfE, 2013a), meaning that approximately six children in every class of 32 will present with a challenging education profile.

- School leaders will need to invest in continuing professional development (CPD) to enable the workforce to adopt a personalised approach to teaching all pupils.

- School leaders must encourage the use of evidence-based teaching methods with clear measureable objectives to enable all children to achieve success.

Implications for SENCos

- SENCos must become more critical of the interventions and approaches used for pupils with SEN and ensure that these have a secure evidence base. This may be a new feature of their role; one which requires time and support from HE establishments.

- For SENCos who are relatively new to their role (post-2009) and who must complete the National Framework Award for SEN Co-ordination, support will be provided in using appropriate school-based research methodology to develop evidence-informed practice. As this qualification is at Masters Level, they will also learn to use a range of literature, policy guidance and research to critically explore the benefits or limitations of different learning approaches or interventions.

Implications for teachers

- Teachers must introduce strategies to capture the personal aspirations of pupils with SEN.

- Teachers must be more reflective in selecting targeted interventions for pupils in the class.

- Teachers need to critically reflect on their teaching and assessment approaches, and to evaluate whether the methods they are adopting are effective in raising attainment and securing better outcomes.

Implications for governors

- Governors will need to be active in ensuring that the aspirations of all pupils are captured and that the curriculum is flexible enough to enable each pupil to realise their potential.

- Governors will need to facilitate more active communication systems between school and home to ensure that there is a joint impetus to realise pupil aspirations.

- Governors will also need to use evidence to inform decisions, especially when these impact on staffing structure and school finance. For example, the role of the teaching assistant might change as a result of SEN reform.

- Governors may be in a position to evaluate strategies to support pupils with SEN which have been effective in neighbouring schools and which could be applied to their home school.

CHAPTER 6
Impartial information, advice and support

Information

The second chapter of the SEN Code of Practice (CoP) focuses on the availability of information and guidance to support children with SEN and disabilities. Section 2.1 states that 'local authorities **must** provide information and advice about matters relating to their SEN or disabilities, including matters relating to health and social care. It must demonstrate joint commissioning with health and social care professionals.'

It recommends that advice should differ according to the person who wishes to access it. For example, a child may wish to obtain information to understand the help available to them. This may differ from the information needed by the parent. This focus on information will hopefully reduce the struggle parents, children and young people often face when trying to obtain answers to their questions.

In Control is a charity which aims to create a fairer society where everyone needing additional support has the right, responsibility and freedom to control that support. It recommends that the information provided should help families to:

- find accurate up-to-date information in one place about what is available to them in their locality
- find out about their options
- find out what is available 'free', what they may be expected to pay for and what this will cost
- understand how the various organisations and professionals involved are working together
- find out where to go for advice and support
- find personal support from someone who knows the system, who can help them interpret information and guide them in the right direction.

Previously, the information provided was inconsistent, with some services providing too much detail, others not enough. The new reforms recommend that this is located in one place and should be called the local offer (LO). For more information on the LO, see Chapter 8.

The information referred to must:

- be impartial and accessible
- apply to the demographics of the area
- be available in multiple formats and languages
- be culturally sensitive
- reflect the diversity of need.

In Control also recommends that it should signpost families to specialist or generic information providers whenever appropriate. The most important aspect is that it should be up to date!

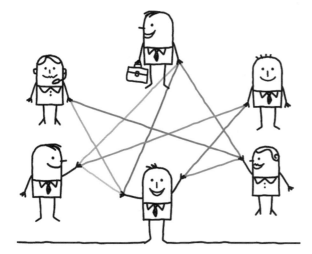

Information exchange

Advice and support

The extent of the reforms in SEN will be a challenge for parents and carers of children with SEN. New assessment and funding arrangements can leave families bewildered and unsure what they must do to secure adequate support for their child. The opportunity to have a personal budget may potentially be very appealing to those families who are eligible; however, the complexities of managing this budget and the necessary accountability can be particularly challenging.

To help parents navigate their way through the new systems, the Government has set aside £30m to fund more than 1800 trained independent supporters (IS). This will equate to 12 advisors per area. Central funding for these IS will be available until March 2016, with the Council for Disabled Children (CDC) overseeing their recruitment and training.

According to the CDC, IS will be used specifically to support parents and children throughout the introduction of the new assessment process and the development of education, health and care (EHC) plans. Support will be provided to:

- new entrants to the system
- children with a statement converting to an EHC plan
- young people with an LDA converting to an EHC plan.

IS are champions drawn from independent voluntary, community and private organisations. They will work with and complement pre-existing local services.

This support is in addition to that offered by parent partnership services (PPS), who will continue to provide free impartial and confidential information, advice and support services to families in every local authority (LA).

Although each LA may have differing demographic needs, their PPS will continue to offer the following services:

The overall aim (of parent partnership services) is to provide a menu of flexible services for parents whose children have SEN in order to empower them to play an active and informed role in their child's education

DfES, 2001

- a confidential helpline
- support for parents and their children in preparing for and attending meetings such as annual reviews and parents' evenings
- help for parents in filling out the appropriate forms, letters and reports relating to their child's needs
- support in resolving disagreements between parents/carers and the school or LA
- signposting other statutory and voluntary services which could support the child or young person, such as Contact-a-Family
- information to help link the family or individual to local parent support groups and forums
- ensuring that parents' and carers' views help inform and influence local policy and practice
- training opportunities for parents and professionals
- working with families of pupils who have been excluded, either temporarily or permanently.

Many parent partnership orgnisations are changing their name to SEND Information, Advice and Support Service (SENDIASS) to reflect this role.

Implications for the leadership team

- School leaders must know how to direct parents to support services such as PPS or IS.
- School leaders must develop good working relationships with support services to resolve issues which may compromise the pupil's progress.

Implications for SENCos

- SENCos should have an active relationship with PPS and IS, who will often take the role of advocate in resolving issues pertinent to the pupil's SEN.

- SENCos should be mindful that the school should present information to parents in a demographically and culturally sensitive manner, such as languages other than English.

- SENCos should respond to advice from the PP or IS to alter the location or structure of reviews so that they are more accessible to individual families.

Implications for teachers

- Teachers will be required to know which support services are available to families or at least direct them to an online source where help can be found.

- Teachers will need to be open to listening to feedback from families, via the PPS or IS, and be willing to act on recommendations aimed at enhancing the learning experience of those with SEN.

Implications for governors

- Governors must ensure that effective relationships and good communication networks are established between the school and local support networks, such as PPS.

- Governors will facilitate discussions regarding recommendations made by support agencies; especially when these relate to individual staff members or the school's structure.

CHAPTER 7
Education, health and social care: working together for positive outcomes

We know that collaboration with colleagues in health and social care is essential if we are to reduce the pressure placed on families and children. It is also necessary if our goal is to provide a seamless service, in which children are not repeatedly assessed and parents perpetually asked the same questions depending on who is collating the information.

However, the challenges we face in working collaboratively are enormous. We have three huge systems, each serving different functions, with their own funding systems and priorities for spending. On a more basic level, each system is based on a different model of service delivery, has a unique operational framework and uses jargon that is often not accessible to the typical public. This said, the new Children and Families Act 2014 has made this collaboration a **priority**, reinforced by the Health and Social Care Act 2012 and the Care Act 2014.

The changes to SEN provision have been introduced at the same time as the NHS and the social care system are also facing radical changes in their finances and service delivery. It can be very difficult to follow the proposed changes to structures and organisation; however, it is important to have an overall understanding of these systems to appreciate how joint commissioning will work in practice.

Joint planning and commissioning framework for children, young people and maternity services, DfES/DH (2006)

Health provision

Clinical commissioning groups (CCGs) are NHS organisations recommended within the Health and Social Care Act 2012 to organise the delivery of NHS services in England. These replace primary care trusts (PCTs). They consist of clinicians from a range of medical professions who 'commission' (or buy) services for their area, such as rehabilitation and learning disability services, from either existing NHS or independent services. CCGs are responsible for arranging emergency and urgent care services within their locality and will commission services for any unregistered patients who live in their area. All GP practices must belong to a CCG.

In order to monitor the commissioning services and ensure that the needs of a specific population (e.g. children with SEN) are being met, health and wellbeing boards have been established in each local authority (LA) in England. These boards aim to ensure that there is no health inequality and that support is not determined by a 'postcode lottery' as previously was the case.

A further stipulation from the Health and Social Care Act 2012 was the appointment of a designated health officer (DHO) for SEN with roles set out in detail in the SEN CoP. The DHO may be an employee of a CCG, an NHS trust, or another provider commissioned by a CCG, NHS England or an LA. The DHO must have a level of expertise that allows them to carry out this role effectively and will have the following responsibilities:

- ensuring that local health services inform the LA of any pre-school children they think may have SEN

- providing a point of contact for the LA and schools seeking health advice on children who may have SEN

- ensuring that other relevant agencies are fully aware of those children who require a jointly commissioned service

- being an advocate for children and young people with SEN

- contributing to the strategic commissioning for SEN

- ensuring positive relationships between local commissioners and education and social care providers, reporting to the CCG executive.

Health services must co-operate with the LA to commission integrated, personalised services and help design the local offer (LO). They must also respond to requests for advice for an education, health and care (EHC) plan within the required 20 weeks and ensure that the healthcare specified in the EHC plan is provided. Additionally, they must contribute to the reviews of children and young people who have EHC plans. The support provided may take the form of medical treatments and/or rehabilitation. This may include occupational therapy, speech and language therapy (SALT) and physiotherapy, a range of nursing support, specialist equipment and wheelchairs.

Social care provision

The Health and Social Care Act 2012 and the Children and Families Act 2014 reiterate the role of social care in supporting children and young people with SEN by providing short breaks, sitters and befrienders, carer support, community activities, specialised equipment and housing adaptations, occupational therapy to enhance independence at home, emergency care, personal care, support for looked-after children with SEN and comprehensive support in the transition from children's to adult services. These services provide a vital contribution to achieving outcomes that can be established across, and impact upon, aspects of education, health and social care.

A relatively simple intervention may have wide-reaching positive benefits. For example, a child with mobility issues could be taught how to transfer independently on and off the toilet with the help of a grab rail and mobility training, which could be reinforced at school. This would encourage a level of independence and enhance the child's self-esteem, while at the same time reducing potential urinary tract infections which can be the result of not toileting frequently enough.

Segregation takes care of itself, collaboration takes work!

Education provision

LAs have been encouraged to come up with innovative ways to undertake joint assessment and service delivery, and have not been given an edict from the Government about how this should be done, allowing local relationships to form and systems to be established reflecting local demographics.

Rochdale LA suggests four stages for joint commissioning:

1 Joint understanding of needs. This involves the identifying and agreeing the needs and goals which will have a positive impact on the children, young people and their families.

2 Joint planning. This requires the creation of a forum to examine the identified needs in the context of the published health and wellbeing strategy and the Children and Young People's Plan. The result of this will be in objectives with clearly measurable outcomes. Some of these outcomes may focus on a vulnerable group, such as service families or looked-after children.

3 Joint delivery. This will involve the implementation of actions and priorities that have been agreed at the planning stage. This may involve the following options:
   • continue with the existing service provision or support
   • redesign existing services
   • decommission existing services
   • procure new or alternative provision.

4 Joint review. This stage focuses on revisiting outcomes, ensuring that performance management from all partners has been engaged in the delivery of outcomes, which will reflect the participation of children, young people, parents and carers.

In addition, outcomes can be established which are holistic and represent the needs of individuals in all aspects of their life. The CDC recommends the following shared outcomes:

○ increasing the proportion of children with SEN whose needs are identified in the early years

○ improving the educational progress and outcomes for children and young people with SEN

○ reducing avoidable unplanned episodes of care in acute hospital services

○ improved family (or patient) experience feedback.

In order to bring health, social care and education providers together in an equitable manner, and in order to ensure that each organisation is accountable for its contribution to meeting the individual's needs, the establishment of a programme board for SEN may be established. This may take responsibility for resolving disputes between the different commissioning parties.

The benefits of joint working for educators are enormous, as social and familial issues which are affecting the child or young person's ability to learn effectively can be addressed by colleagues in social care, and medical issues can be addressed in a contextually appropriate manner. For example, physiotherapy, which is health-funded, could be provided in the school to enable a young person with physical needs to be included in the class PE lesson. A child with significant attention/concentration difficulties due to poor sleeping habits could be supported by professionals in social care who could work with the family in developing consistent bedtime routines.

If routine therapy were to be cross-referenced with the national curriculum it has the potential to reduce the pressure on pupil time, curriculum content and therapy resources.

Mackey & McQueen, 1998

Activity: Working together (1)

To appreciate the dynamic nature of collaboration between education, health and social care professionals, consider the following case study.

Case study: Chloe

Name: Chloe, aged 13

School: Attends mainstream secondary school

Year group: Currently in Year 8

Medical history

Chloe was born full-term, following an emergency caesarean section owing to complications during labour. She was slightly late in achieving her developmental milestones, preferring to sit and watch, rather than interact with those around her, ultimately walking at 20 months.

By the time Chloe reached the age of two, her mother was concerned that her language was not developing well, despite her seeming to be very aware of, if not sensitive to, sounds. Following assessment by the multi-disciplinary team located in the Child Development Centre, Chloe was diagnosed with autism.

At the age of eight, Chloe was also diagnosed with Crohn's disease. This restricts her diet and can lead to painful symptoms. She can occasionally be incontinent, which distresses her enormously, although she can manage to change herself when needed. She has to have medication at school for this, and so has a healthcare plan in place. She sometimes needs an enema last thing at night.

She also has very bad eczema, but this is managed by her mother at home. Chloe's eczema is worse when she feels stressed.

Current presentation

Chloe can communicate, although conversations are factual and concrete. Chloe's social skills often feel rote-learned; she is very polite and at times over formal. She needs a clear routine, especially around meal times and can't bear to be hungry. Her behaviour can be challenging when she is hungry or feels out-of-sync, but as she gets older she is getting better at asking for time-out in a quiet place.

She can struggle to fall or remain asleep throughout the night, and this can be disruptive for her mother and sister.

Activity: Working together (2)

Social history

Chloe lives with her mother and younger sister. Her mum finds it hard to give Chloe access to social opportunities, due to what she feels are Chloe's unusual behaviours. This causes her to be a little over protective. Chloe's younger sister (Poppy, aged nine) does not have autism, but her language was also delayed.

Chloe lives with her mother and sister in a housing association property in a central location. Chloe's father left shortly after Chloe was diagnosed with autism and has little contact with the family.

Education

At school Chloe is an accepted member of her class. Her form tutor is aware that she is occasionally teased, but Chloe is mainly oblivious to this. She has two friends, Millie and Lauren, and all three go to Learning Support together for extra support in English and maths.

Chloe's learning is significantly delayed and school staff don't feel they really know what makes her tick. It can be hard to predict what she will struggle with and therefore how to support her effectively. She seems to have some memory problems and maths is a real issue, even more so than her literacy.

Chloe loves making things and drawing. She is particularly interested in wildlife, especially birds, and does brilliant illustrations of them.

She hates noisy places and anywhere with strip lighting, which makes one or two of the classrooms difficult for her. She likes to have an allocated seat in a classroom with plenty of personal space. She would rather not do paired or group work and can be quite vocal about this.

She would always rather spend her lunch break in Learning Support, hating the crowds and noise of the school dining room.

Activity: Working together (3)

Can you highlight Chloe's key needs and identify **who** should address these?

Education	Health	Social care

How do you think that collaborative working will help Chloe?

_____

_____

_____

_____

_____

Answers on pages 97–98.

Implications for the leadership team

● Strong leadership and senior management support are key drivers in the development and implementation of multi-agency and multi-disciplinary working, particularly in relation to the development of links between services.

● There is evidence that schools with the strongest and most embedded multi-agency working practices also have inclusion or SEN strategies that are clearly linked to local and national strategies and policies (Lewis et al, 2010).

Implications for SENCos

● Some schools have separate strategies for selected childhood conditions with a higher prevalence, such as autism. It is good practice that these strategies reflect multi-agency involvement so that consistent and supportive advice is provided to pupils and their families.

● It is recommended that support for pupils with sensory impairments, such as vision and hearing impairments, reflect multi-agency working.

Implications for teachers

● Teachers will be able to collaborate with professionals in health and social care to support pupils with SEN in the classroom.

● Working more closely with other professionals will increase awareness and learning between health and education staff. This includes mental health services.

● Effective liaison can ensure increased access to health, social care and mental health services and a greater understanding of the services available.

● Teachers will be able to ensure that health and social care staff have a greater understanding of the school context and the impact it may have on children's physical and mental health, and home context.

Implications for governors

● Governors may be involved in multi-agency planning around a pupil with SEN in their school. It is important that multi-agency groups do not get too big, lose focus or become disconnected from other systems and processes. Governors have a role in ensuring that this does not happen.

● Challenges to implementing child-centred models include a lack of funding to allow time for taking on these additional duties, which can lead to staff being disinclined to take on this role. Governors have a role in addressing this reluctance.

CHAPTER 8
The local offer

As of 1 September 2014 every local authority (LA) is expected to produce a local offer (LO). This is a central online information service which outlines many different services, from training, travel arrangements and social care, to special education provision. The section on SEN must involve children, young people and parents in reviewing and developing appropriate provision and will include support groups and partner services. Information will be published in different formats to accommodate those:

- who do not have internet access
- whose first language is not English
- who have a visual impairment
- who have a learning difficulty.

The aim of the LO is to improve choice and transparency for families about the services available to them. It will also be an important tool for professionals to use, as it will allow them to understand the full range of services and provision in the local area.

Regulations have been established to ensure that the LO includes a wide range of independent and impartial advice. These have been developed following intense scrutiny and consultation. The starting point for preparing the offer is extensive dialogue between the LA, children and young people with SEN and their parents and carers to identify the sorts of information they require, what format this should be in and how it should be presented. There should be evidence that this consultation has occurred, including public comments.

The LO will represent services provided from three sectors: education, health and social care. It will reflect collaborative working between health, social care and education providers. It should also indicate joint commissioning of services for children and young people with SEN and disabilities.

The health authority's contribution to the LO should include:

- the therapy services available and how to access these, including any criteria that must be satisfied before this provision can be provided
- the availability of mental health services such as Child and Adolescent Mental Health Services (CAMHS) and how to access these, including any criteria that must be satisfied before they can be provided

O services for relevant early years providers, schools and post-16 institutions to assist them in supporting children and young people with medical conditions.

The social care contribution to the LO should include:

O services provided in accordance with Section 17 of the Children Act 1989; this refers to procedures to ensure the safeguarding and welfare of vulnerable children and young people

O the arrangements for supporting young people when moving from children's to adult services

O support for young people in planning for and assisting with independent living.

The LO must cover services available to those with SEN from the age of 0–25 years. It should span a range of special educational provision, including:

O relevant early years education providers

O maintained schools, including those that have provisions made in any separate unit

O academies

O non-maintained special schools

O post-16 institutions

O institutions approved under Section 41 of the Act; these include independent special schools and special post-16 institutions

O pupil referral units (PRUs)

O persons commissioned by the LA to support children and young people with SEN

O the special educational provision the LA expects to be made outside of its area.

One section of the LO should be dedicated to transport issues and the necessary criteria for supporting pupils when travelling to schools or colleges. This should indicate whether the service is free or has a cost attached, and what that cost may be.

The LO should highlight those support services available to families which may be offered by independent providers or charities. It will include links to support groups and parent advocacy services such as parent partnership services (PPS). Opportunities for positive and negative feedback will be an integral part of the LO so that services can evolve and grow according to local demographic demands.

The new funding arrangements for supporting children and young people with SEN should also be transparent and be part of the LO so that parents can see how resources have been distributed. This will provide information about how schools can use their notional SEN and higher level SEN budgets to provide 'additional and different' support and resources for those with SEN. These should align to each school's SEN policy, which seeks to explain how the school will support pupils with SEN.

The LO will help schools explain the types of additional and/or different arrangements they will make for pupils with SEN. These could relate to all aspects of school life: in the classroom, during the school day and in activities beyond the school day.

According to the CDC, the information provided under the category of 'additional and different' could include arrangements made for:

- teaching and learning

- assessment

- the ways in which access to the curriculum is facilitated

- specialist expertise, within and beyond the school

- pastoral support

- intervention programmes over and above high quality classroom teaching for all pupils, such as booster programmes, resilience modules, oracy or social skills groups

- equipment that schools provide

- staffing arrangements to promote access; for example, a teacher to co-ordinate transition between Years 6 and 7.

Council for Disabled Children, 2012

Further information can also be included that reflects the graduated approach to assessing individual need: Assess, Plan, Do, Review. This may include the following:

http://www.councilfordisabledchildren.org.uk/media/246954/local%20offer.pdf

O Assessment
- These are procedures that will help to identify the particular SEN of a child or young person.
- This will involve the child or young person and their family.

O Planning
- This is how to secure the services, provision and equipment required by children and young people with SEN.

O Intervention/support
- This is the school or setting's approach to teaching, learning and development of children and young people with SEN.
- It will include the adaptations which have been implanted in the curriculum or provision.
- Information will be given on the additional learning support available to children and young people with SEN.
- It will include details of the activities are available for children and young people with SEN in addition to the curriculum.
- It will show how the emotional and social development of children and young people with SEN will be supported and improved.

O Review
- This will indicate how the school will review and evaluate the outcomes identified for the pupil with SEN, ideally including them in this review.

O Transition
- This is the support available to help the individual move between phases of education and in preparing for adulthood.

O Teacher continuing professional development (CPD)
- This will include information on how the expertise of staff will be enhanced to support those with SEN.

The LO should make services more transparent. Over the past ten years school staff have developed their expertise in addressing the needs of pupils with SEN; however, much of this is covert and embedded into daily practice. This can leave parents feeling very confused about how their child is being supported. Limitations in home–school communication can exacerbate concerns, especially when the pupil enters secondary school. A lack of communication can lead to parents' seeking their own solutions to addressing their child's needs. This may lead to embarking on interventions which are expensive and look credible, and which may provide some 'guarantees' of success. However, these are often provided outside school, and may not translate into the curriculum. By explaining the pathways offered to pupils in school, many of the fears and anxieties experienced by parents and carers can be allayed. See also the example of support available for dyslexia on page 58.

The LO has considerable benefits and according to the Council for Disabled Children has the potential to:

- ○ provide clarity and confidence for parents
- ○ instigate earlier intervention
- ○ reduce the need for numerous assessments
- ○ improve family wellbeing by providing short breaks
- ○ identify need and gaps in provision
- ○ provide an evidence base for improving progress and securing better outcomes, at school and local level
- ○ help children and young people with SEN to access leisure facilities.

The local offer

The most important facet of this information portal is that it should be up to date! This will require considerable on-going dialogue with multiple services, and as such requires a full-time commitment. Ultimately, it should be a dynamic site which hosts open and honest dialogue between service users and providers alike. It is up to LAs and parents groups to rise to the challenge that the LO presents.

The Offer is an attempt to restructure the relationships and culture in an overarching framework which seeks to end the conflict on SEND provision between parents and statutory authorities through encouraging co-production of services.

Lamb, 2013

Special educational needs and disabilities (SEND) - local offer

 What is the local offer?
Find out what the local offer is, what information is in it and how to use it.

 SEND - information and support
Find out about the parent partnership service and other support that is available.

 SEND - education
Find out about special educational needs in primary and secondary schools as well as in early years.

 SEND - health
Find out about healthcare provision and services.

 SEND - care
Information about care can be found here.

 SEND - statutory assessments
Find out about the statement and assessment process.

 SEND - moving into adult life
Find out about the post-16 options available and the young person's local offer.

 SEND - transport
Find out when transport is provided and what the independent travel training scheme is.

 SEND - what's in my local offer?
Find out what's in your local offer including the site map and the young person's local offer.

Example of a local offer website

The North Yorkshire County Council website uses landing page symbols to assist with signposting and directing people to relevant information. These symbols were originally created by Liverpool City Council and were thoroughly tested by users.

http://www.northyorks.gov.uk/article/23542/ SEND---local-offer

Summary table: the local offer

The local offer will...	The local offer will not...
Provide information regarding local services available for children and young people with SEN from the ages of 0–25	Be a directory of services
Link the user to relevant information appropriate to their initial question or search	Base information on the LA's choice of terms (i.e. SpLD instead of dyslexia or dysgraphia instead of handwriting difficulties)
Provide details on schools and colleges regarding how they run	Recommend one school or college over another
Refer to current legislation	Only provide information on statutory obligations
Reflect children's, parents' and carers' perspectives	Have a corporate feel
Provide effective signposting to support services, which may be independent, charitable or authority-commissioned	Recommend one service over another
Inform joint commissioning	Provide a list of services offered by social services and health without making links to integrated working
Provide a positive view of SEN focusing on strengths	Focus on the disability, and those with an identified condition, disorder or special need
Filter out information that is not useful	Be out of date
Reflect constant partnership with children and parents/carers	Be a simple web-based solution
Empower parents to select services appropriate for their child/young person	Recommend services which have been established by the LA
Be user-led	Be service-led

Implications for the leadership team

- School leaders must publish a clear SEN strategy which aligns with information provide on the LO.

- School policies must also align with information placed on the LO.

- School leaders should contribute to the LO and be active in ensuring that it reflects current practice.

- School leaders will need to encourage a culture shift so that staff work more closely with families to refine, alter or adapt the interventions provided within the school.

- The new relationship with health and social care professionals will mean that education providers will be working with these agencies, especially in the delivery of an EHC plan. School leaders will need to help ensure there is clarity on the parameters and responsibilities of each agency.

Implications for SENCos

- SENCos will be actively involved in ensuring that the school's SEN policies and strategies are transparent and clear.

- SENCos will work with the school leadership and parents to align school practice with recommendations stipulated in the LO.

Implications for teachers

- The class teacher becomes the conduit through which SEN decisions are effected, with enhanced responsibility for the success of pupils with SEN.

- Teachers will need to know their children well and take overall responsibility for enabling pupils with SEN to achieve established objectives, while teaching assistants will support other learners.

- Plans for pupils will need to be aspirational, time measured and carefully monitored. As details regarding how the schools supports pupils with SEN will be publically available, teachers must ensure that the rhetoric becomes a reality.

Implications for governors

- Governors must be actively involved in ensuring that school practices are transparent and resource allocation is fair and appropriate. Funding is finite, so governors and school leaders must be accountable for how it is shared out.

- Governors must take responsibility for monitoring and reporting on the impact and effectiveness of a changed SEN legislative system.

- Governors should consider how the school judges whether any additional support offered has had an impact on the child or young person's educational progress.

CHAPTER 9
Early years

The Children and Families Act 2014 covers children and young people from birth to 25 years. The outworking of this, through the Code of Practice (CoP), emphasises the early identification of children's needs. This is underpinned by the considerable research that demonstrates how positive outcomes can be achieved by the provision of early intervention to those who are vulnerable to following a different developmental path (Barnett, 2011; Guralnick, 2011).

Parents often know their child best, and may express concerns regarding their child's development from birth, especially when they have more than one child and are therefore able to compare the child's development against another sibling. Health professionals are usually the first to learn of parents' concerns and need to work with parents and relevant agencies such as childminders or nurseries to monitor and support the child's development, providing recommendations regarding interventions where appropriate. However, this concept of 'wait and see' should not result in a substantial widening of the gap between the child's development and that of their peers to the extent that the child is at a disadvantage on entry to school.

However, initial concerns may also be raised by someone other than the parent and the CoP also states that if a health professional believes that a young child has a developmental delay or difference, they must inform the child's parents and bring the child to the attention of the appropriate local authority (LA). The health body must also give the parents the opportunity to discuss this opinion and let them know about any voluntary organisations that are likely to be able to provide advice or assistance. This includes the educational advice, guidance and interventions such as Portage (a home visiting educational service for pre-school children with additional support needs and their families) to be put in place at an early point and before the child starts school.

National Portage Association http://www.portage.org.uk/

Early years practitioners are in also in an excellent position to identify aspects of development that are different to those of other children of a similar age. This is not always obvious to parents, who perhaps may only have one child or a limited understanding of developmental norms. By setting targets for these children it is possible to boost the skills required for future learning and social interaction. For example, we know that early intervention for children with oral language difficulties is effective and can successfully support the skills which underpin reading comprehension (Fricke et al, 2013).

In order to set the standards for the learning, development and care of children from birth to five years, all early years providers must have arrangements in place to support children with SEN or disabilities. This will require maintained nursery schools to identify a member of staff to act as

Special Educational Needs Co-ordinator (SENCo), who **must** be a qualified teacher. Other providers (in group provision), including childminders who work within agencies, are also expected to identify a SENCo, although these are not obliged to be qualified teachers. They will be supported by area SENCos who will also provide assistance in the child's transition to school.

There is a new stipulation in the CoP to evaluate each child's progress at key points throughout the pre-school years; in particular, progress at the age of two years, and then again at five. Previous practice saw health practitioners assessing children, and educators doing the same, with little liaison between the two. This is being replaced in 2015 by the **integrated health check** at two years of age. This will:

94% of children who achieve a good level of development at age five go on to achieve the expected levels for reading at Key Stage 1, and they are five times more likely to achieve the highest level.

Pupils who start off in the bottom 20% of attainment at age five are six times more likely to be in the bottom 20% at Key Stage 1 compared to their peers.

DfE, 2014b

O identify the child's progress, strengths and needs at this age, in order to promote positive outcomes in health and wellbeing, learning and development

O enable appropriate intervention and support for children and their families, where progress is less than expected

O generate information which can be used to plan services and help reduce inequality in children's outcomes.

2014 saw changes in the early years foundation stage (EYFS) framework with a reduction from 69 stipulated learning goals to 17. The new framework reflects the CoP's requirements for young children with SEN. The CoP encourages settings to consider the needs of children within four broad categories:

1 communication and interaction
2 cognition and learning
3 social, emotional and mental health
4 sensory and/or physical needs.

The EYFS areas of learning can be aligned to these CoP categories to enable practitioners to determine the key areas of developmental concern as follows:

CoP SEN category	EYFS heading	Areas of learning
Communication and interaction	Communication and language development	Listening and attention Understanding Speaking
Sensory and/or physical needs	Physical development	Moving and handling Health and self-care
Social, emotional and mental health	Personal, social and emotional development	Self-confidence and self-awareness Managing feelings and behaviour Making relationships
Cognition and learning	Specific areas of learning	Literacy development: reading and writing Mathematical development: number, shape, space and measure Understanding of the world Expressive arts and design

Of course, children's needs do not always fit into neat categories, and there will be an overlap in many areas; the ultimate focus should be to consider the family's needs and the best ways to support them. This helps in the planning and provision of appropriate resources.

On identification of need, early years settings must then consider appropriate evidence-based interventions with a proven record of success. This may be an alien concept to many practitioners but with a growing culture of accountability across all dimensions of service provision it is becoming an essential component of early years practice.

Assess, Plan, Do, Review

The process of Assess, Plan, Do, Review applies to pre-school settings in order to ensure that the child will get the best start. This will require closer collaboration between professionals within child development centres and setting providers. It will require early years practitioners to be active in understanding differing learning profiles and how to address or remediate these.

As with school-based practice, the categories of Early Years Action and Early Years Action Plus have been withdrawn and a stepped approach to addressing the child's needs is encouraged. To provide consistency in support, children with complex SEN can have an education, health and care (EHC) plan during their pre-school years and two-year-olds with EHC plans, statements of SEN or who are eligible for Disability Living Allowance are now entitled to 570 hours per year of funded early education. This is an extension to the entitlement that three- and four-year-olds have enjoyed for a number of years and is in addition to funding which gave 15 hours of free early years provision for vulnerable two-year-olds.

The increased emphasis on identifying clear outcomes for young children with SEN may challenge those working in the various settings. Detailed knowledge of child development will be required in order to identify those children who require extra support in their early years. The Government has agreed that further training will be required for many early years providers and in September 2013 launched further courses for early years teachers and educators.

Examples of evidence-based interventions

Communication and interaction

Koegel LK, Koegel RL, Ashbaugh K & Bradshaw J (2014). The importance of early identification and intervention for children with or at risk for autism spectrum disorders. *International Journal of Speech and Language Pathology*, 16 (1): 50–56.

Polišenská K & Kapalková S (2014). Language profiles in children with Down Syndrome and children with Language Impairment: Implications for early intervention. *Research in Developmental Disabilities*, 35 (2): 373–382.

Cognition and learning

Fawcett AJ, Lee R & Nicolson R (2014). Sustained benefits of a multi-skill intervention for pre-school children at risk of literacy difficulties. *Asia Pacific Journal of Developmental Differences*, 1 (1): 62–77.

Praet M & Desoete A (2014). Enhancing young children's arithmetic skills through non-intensive, computerised kindergarten interventions: A randomised controlled study. *Teaching and Teacher Education*, 39: 56–65.

Social, emotional and mental health

Graziano PA, Slavec J, Hart K, Garcia A & Pelham WE (2014). Improving school readiness in preschoolers with behavior problems: Results from a summer treatment program. *Journal of Psychopathology and Behavioral Assessment*. http://link.springer.com/article/10.1007%2Fs10862-014-9418-1.

McCabe PC & Altamura M (2011). Empirically valid strategies to improve social and emotional competence of preschool children. *Psychology in the Schools*, 48 (5): 513–540.

Sensory and/or physical needs

Ziviani J, Feeney R, Rodger S & Watter P (2010). Systematic review of early intervention programmes for children from birth to nine years who have a physical disability. *Australian Occupational Therapy Journal*, 57: 210–223.

Logan SW, Robinson LE, Wilson AE & Lucas WA (2012). Getting the fundamentals of movement: A meta-analysis of the effectiveness of motor skill interventions in children. *Child: Care, Health and Development*, 38: 305–315.

Changes to EYFS 2014

- Childminder agencies now must to adhere to the SEN CoP (2014).
- Additional recommendations may require staff to take further appropriate training and professional development regarding child development and SEN.
- There is now a requirement for those childminders and assistants who may be left in sole charge of children to hold a paediatric first aid qualification. The removal of the requirement for first aid training has yet to be LA-approved.
- Early years teacher status has been introduced and is equal to qualified teacher status (QTS).
- Funding will be available to support graduates becoming early years teachers.
- The requirement for a named practitioner to be responsible for behaviour management in every setting has been removed, encouraging universal responsibility. The new wording states 'providers are responsible for managing behaviour in an appropriate way'.
- The requirement for providers to follow their legal responsibilities under the Equality Act 2010 has been included.
- Providers must ensure that they take reasonable steps to ensure that staff are not exposed to risks, and must be able to demonstrate how they are managing risk. This may relate to a child's behavioural or medical issue.
- The requirement for an equal opportunities policy has been removed, due to references to the Equality Act 2010.
- Changes to SENCo arrangements mean that maintained nursery schools must each identify a member of staff to act as SENCo and other providers are expected to identify a SENCo for their group.

Implications for the leadership team

- Setting leaders must use their best endeavours to monitor all children in their care and to identify those whose development may be divergent, delayed or different.

- Setting leaders must make sure that any child with an identified SEN gets the support they need.

- Setting leaders must ensure that children with SEN have access to and are engaged in activities alongside children without SEN.

- Setting leaders must designate a SENCo who, in a maintained setting, must be a qualified teacher. Childminders are encouraged to identify a person to act as a SENCo and those in an agency or network may wish to share the role between them.

- Setting leaders must inform parents when they are concerned that a child may have SEN.

- Setting leaders must inform parents when making special educational provision for a child with SEN.

- Setting leaders must consider the skill sets of staff and identify further training needs.

Implications for early years SENCos

- In collaboration with the setting leader, the early years (EY) SENCo must provide clear admission arrangements for children with SEN. This should be collated in an accessibility plan.

- EY SENCos should ensure that steps are taken to prevent children with SEN from being treated less favourably than others.

- EY SENCos should ensure that all practitioners in the setting understand their own responsibilities in relation to children with SEN as well as the setting's approach to identifying and meeting SEN.

- EY SENCos must advise and support colleagues in enhancing the potential of children with SEN.

- EY SENCos must liaise with professionals or agencies beyond the setting; for example, therapists in child development centres.

- EY SENCos will be responsible for explaining the new SEN framework and duties to staff (and volunteers), explaining the removal of Early Years Action and Early Years Action Plus and applying a new single-stage graduated approach for identifying and meeting children's SEN.

- EY SENCos will be responsible for bringing children identified with SEN to the attention of the LA, and for signposting families to support and mediation services such as parent partnership services (PPS).

Implications for early years practitioners

- Early years practitioners (EYPs) should look carefully at all aspects of a child's learning and development to establish whether any delay is related to learning English as an additional language or arises from SEN or disability.

- EYPs must review children's progress and provide parents with a short written summary of their child's development, focusing in particular on communication and language, physical development and personal, social and emotional development.

- EYPs must inform the EY SENCo where a child's progress is slower than expected.

- If there are significant emerging concerns (or identified SEN or disability) the EYP, together with the EY SENCo, should develop a targeted plan to support the child. Plans must focus on outcomes to meet children's SEN and adopt a graduated approach involving Assess, Plan, Do, Review.

Implications for early years governors

❶ EY governors need to be aware that the full range of statutory requirements, as stipulated in the EYFS statutory framework booklet, is non-negotiable.

❶ EY governors should also ensure that practitioners are able to implement the EYFS and SEN CoP.

❶ EY governors should be aware of their duty to arrange for practitioners responsible for the completion of the early years foundation stage profile (EYFSP) to attend these LA moderation activities every year. They are crucial if school EYFSP data are to be accurate.

CHAPTER 10
Schools

The new legislation emphasises the importance of improving outcomes by establishing high aspirations and expectations for pupils with SEN **regardless of their learning need or disability**. This requires a shift in thinking for many who have developed an understanding of pupil performance based on an understanding of their 'condition'. This is a legacy from the past when developmental differences were felt to have originated from an intrinsic deficit. This biomedical approach placed the learning difficulty squarely on the shoulders of the individual with little consideration for the other influences on the pupil's ability to learn.

As pupils with a wide array of SEN accessed mainstream school, teachers were led to an understanding of the 'condition', how it presented and what to do to support the pupil amid others who were typically developing. Continuing professional development (CPD) often focused on the symptoms, which were typically negative, omitting to include the individual's abilities and skills, and grouping the pupil into a heterogeneous group of those with similar difficulties.

The focus on childhood conditions such as attention deficit (hyperactivity) disorder (ADHD), dyslexia and autism gave the pupil a label that began to be linked to resources and funding. This caused parents to fight to obtain a diagnosis in order for their child to receive extra support as they struggled to fit into a typically developing peer group.

Labels are for jars not people

The problem with these labels was that they stuck and prevented pupils from 'growing'. This led to an ethos of low aspirations as the pupils' level of performance was construed as 'as good as can be expected'. Lamb (DCSF, 2009) challenged this negative assessment of pupils' performance and the low aspirations of teachers for these pupils.

The new Code of Practice (CoP) provides regulations which should quash such a limited approach. It recommends that teachers should identify pupils' strengths and abilities, rather than focusing on their difficulties and limitations. From this optimistic position, it is recommended that outcomes should stablished which reflect high, aspirational expectations and ensure that the individual maximises ir learning potential. The CoP therefore places less emphasis on the cause of the learning difficulty l more on the functional and learning needs of the individual.

To reduce the allocation of further categories, the new legislation has removed the stages of School Action (SA) and School Action Plus (SA+). Although these categories were 'softer' than previous classifications, they still led to a lowering of expectations, and were used as an excuse as to why pupils did not achieve significant progress. In reality, these terms were adding yet another label to the individual. For example, 'Susan has severe dyslexia and is currently supported at School Action Plus.'

A further derogatory classification that has been removed from the new legislation is the term behavioural, emotional and social difficulties (BESD). This has been replaced by social, mental and emotional health (SMEH). This indicates that there is an underlying reason for an individual's conduct, shifting the emphasis to the cause rather than the individual's negative actions. These causes may be external to the pupil, such as the home context, low self-esteem, teaching methods and so on.

The SA and SA+ categories are replaced by a **graduated approach**, which is intended to encourage a focus on capabilities and identifying individual's strengths and abilities, before identifying aspirations (Norwich, 2014). A central feature of this approach is the value of human diversity. This approach recognises that a child or young person's development is determined by a combination of biological, psychological and social factors.

This approach has links to the biopsychosocial model adopted by the International Classification of Functioning, Disability and Health (ICF) (WHO, 2007), a framework which considers the multiple factors that impact on the individual's ability to function independently and learn. The ICF has proved a useful model and can be used to understand what makes an individual tick! These facets may include the classroom or school environment, the knowledge that the teacher has about the way a pupil learns, the teacher's ability to differentiate material, the size of the class, the relationships within the class, the pupil's motivation to learn and the support the pupil has external to school. All these variables impact on the pupil's ability to learn.

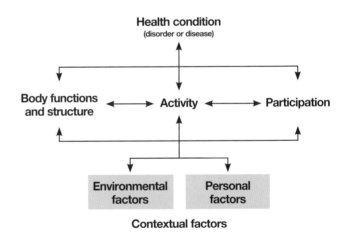

Biopsychosocial model adopted by the International Classification of Functioning, Disability and Health (ICF) (WHO, 2007)

The ICF identifies the following six facets to be considered in order to determine the influences which are helping or hindering the pupil's capacity to learn:

1 **Body structure/health condition.** This refers to the physiological, anatomical and psychological changes to the body which can affect the body's structure, movement, perceptual and sensory development. A child with cerebral palsy, for example, may have limited use of one limb or distorted speech. These structural differences may be impossible to change, so teachers would have to differentiate material to accommodate these. In this case, the teacher could introduce the pupil to a one-handed typing programme to improve writing speed, legibility and output.

2 **Personal factors.** This explains what makes the child tick: their temperament, motivation and moods. If the teacher is able to understand the individual learning styles of their pupils, and be flexible enough to utilise materials which fully involve them, this can play a huge part in maximising their learning potential. To fully engage pupils, teachers must find out their interests, set appropriate challenges, value their response, have high expectations, provide choice and above all develop an effective relationship.

3 **Activities.** This relates to functional and educational activities that an individual can undertake independent of others. For example, a pupil with ADHD may be able to engage in an online learning programme concentrating very well, but may be unable to do the same when working in a small group.

4 **Participation.** This relates to activities which take place with or are demanded by others. These require compliance, co-operation and an interpersonal relationship. *Some* students with autism may find this particularly challenging due to difficulties in understanding meaning, verbal emphasis, body language, facial expressions, sarcasm and humour. However, *other* students with autism may be able to undertake the same task completely independently.

5 **Environment.** This relates to factors within the environment that can impact on the individual's ability to learn. This can refer to factors such noise levels, the amount of visual 'clutter' in the classroom and the ambient temperature. Increasingly we are looking to make classrooms more learner-friendly. This is especially important for those with more 'hidden' difficulties, such as specific learning difficulties (SpLD) including dyslexia and developmental co-ordination disorder (DCD, formerly dyspraxia), and those with sensory processing differences. The creation of 'dyslexia-friendly' classrooms was encouraged following the Rose Review (DfES, 2006); however, this can be extended further to help all pupils with visual and auditory processing differences, and in doing so facilitate excellent learning. For more information see also the example of 'The sensory smart classroom' below.

6 **Context.** These are variables which can impact on an individual's ability to learn in either the learning context or the home. For example, a teacher may set work at too high or too low a level; a pupil may be vulnerable to bullying and feel anxious and stressed in certain lessons; or a pupil may not be able to get to sleep at home and subsequently feel lethargic at school.

The sensory smart classroom

Alteration	Rationale
School signage is clear and uses dyslexia-friendly fonts such as Comic Sans or Ariel	Assists with finding location of rooms
Primary schools: clear labels are used around the classroom and school with symbols such as Communicate: In Print or Widgit where appropriate	Consistent use of symbols associated with words can enhance whole-word recognition
Secondary schools: colour-coded zoned areas around the school or symbol on the door highlight subject specialities, such as mathematics, English	Enhances orientation around large secondary school buildings
Forward-facing tables and chairs. Seating plans can also be useful	Assists with visual focus

Alteration	Rationale
Lesson objectives are clearly displayed at the front of the class	Helps pupils understand focus of lesson
Whiteboard tinted to reduce glare of black text on white background	Reduces the blurring of letters for those with dyslexia and visual stress
Large lesson segmentation dial on wall in front of pupils	Pupils can see how the lesson is divided; for example, 5 minutes: listening; 10 minutes: discussion; 10 minutes: independent writing; 35 minutes: group activity
Alphabet arc	Helps pupils 'see' the position of the letters in the alphabet even when they are no longer in front of them
Visual timetable or timeline	Uses pictures to break down steps of a task or a routine throughout the day
Angled writing board	Improves visual acuity and focus. It also places the wrist in a good position for writing
Reading windows	Help reduce the amount of text seen on a page at any one time
Blinds to filter external stimuli	Reduce distractibility caused by unexpected external stimuli, such as traffic, trees moving in the wind, outside activities
Alternatives to written recording are offered, access to assistive software or hardware where appropriate	Reduce fatigue for those who struggle to write (e.g. laptop, iPad, Dictaphone)
Ergonomic tools	Encourage a more functional and effective writing grip (e.g. S Move pens, PenAgain, ring pen, easy grip pencils etc.)
Traffic light planners/cards: red = I need help; amber = I am a little unsure; green = I know what I am supposed to do	Indicate pupil's level of understanding. Will help teachers to know which pupils need more support. Can also be used by pupils who struggle with a noisy environment, with colours indicating their level of tolerance
Traffic light poster on wall next to whiteboard	Reminds pupils and teachers to use system for expressing levels of understanding
Learning mats (all subjects)	Indicate any key words or formulae required for that subject or lesson
Key words on whiteboard	Reminds students of terms pertinent to the lesson
Buff-coloured lined paper or exercise books	Enhances readability of print
Strategic location of displays behind students	Reduces visual distractibility
Use of personal word books	Help pupils who struggle to spell or find the right word for a descriptor

Alteration	Rationale
Privacy boards, ear defenders, coloured overlays (all context dependent)	Sensory filters to sift out visual and auditory information when these are becoming a distraction
Tennis ball rockers for chairs, move 'n' sit cushions (both context dependent)	Strategies for maintaining attention. Rocking stimulates the vestibular sense, textured cushions stimulate the proprioceptors to maintain sitting position
Worksheets: in general 'less is more', text to be left aligned, no words to be split over lines	Good use of white space and limited text assists with reading; split words afford a huge challenge to pupils who are dyslexic
Where possible, use lower case rather than capital letters	Especially helpful for children with dyslexia
Avoid using italics and underlining wherever possible	Helps with visual focus and legibility
ACE Spelling Dictionary	Helps with spelling (uses phonetic spelling to source correct term)
Decluttered classroom (avoid washing lines)	Reduces visual distractibility
Consideration is given to the potential for auditory distraction, for example, sound carrying from other areas	Regular audits of the classroom can help reduce visual and auditory distractions, which may significantly affect pupils with sensory processing differences
No fly posting: displays on designated boards only	Learning walls celebrate achievement without becoming 'busy' or distracting
Analogue and digital clocks displayed side by side for reinforcement	Reinforces skills for learning to tell the time

The consideration of these variables can result in shifting the focus from an attempt to alter the individual to changing the environment, task, learning materials, teaching approach and lesson style.

Consider the following example which depicts Sally and James, two young people with a similar physical presentation. This shows that differences in context, personality, support networks and classroom dynamics can significantly affect the outcomes for each pupil.

Variables/influences	Sally	James
Health condition	Sally is 10 years old and has cerebral palsy.	James is 10 years old and has cerebral palsy.

Variables/influences	Sally	James
Body functions	Sally has restricted movement down the right side of her body. She has little functional grip in her right hand. She is mobile using a tripod (albeit slowly) and only uses a wheelchair for longer distances such as school trips.	James has restricted movement down the right side of his body. He has little functional grip in his right hand. James is able to transfer and move independently (with care) at home. However, at school he prefers to use a wheelchair and relies on his friends to move him around.
Personal factors	Sally is highly motivated and determined that her motor weaknesses will not stop her from participating at school. She already has high aspirations to study geography, partially influenced by the family's love of flora, fauna and the outdoor life.	James loves video games and spends hours gaming with his brothers and friends. He finds much of his school work irrelevant and has aspirations to be an expert in the 'Call of Duty' video game.
Activity	Sally is determined to be as independent as possible and can undertake all self-care activities with minimal support, as her mother has adapted her clothes (following advice from her occupational therapist) so that dressing and undressing for PE at school is efficient. She has good literacy and numeracy skills and maintains the same pace of learning as her peers. She is learning to type, having been introduced to a one-handed method.	James is capable of reading and writing; however, his writing is laboured, heavy and often illegible. He has a keyboard but is reluctant to use it in class. James relies on the class teaching assistant to affirm what he is expected to do.
Participation	Sally loves group activities and enjoys school. She has a strong supportive group of friends who have known her since she was small.	James is quite passive in group activities. He needs considerable prompts to participate in group work and can appear lazy and unmotivated.
Environment	Sally attends a small village primary school. All school staff have received training on cerebral palsy from the physiotherapist and occupational therapist based at the local child development centre. Every member of staff participated in this training and all know how to enable Sally to be as independent as possible. The school had previously been adapted to accommodate a young boy who required wheelchair access.	James attends a large primary school in the suburbs of a large city. It is an old building set on many floors. Extra stair rails have been fitted to improve access, but the school are awaiting funds to install a through-floor lift. James's teacher is new and has limited knowledge and experience in supporting a child with a physical need. The class is large, with 35 pupils; 35% of these do not have English as their first language.

Variables/influences	Sally	James
Environment	Sally has minimal additional resources to support her, other than an angled writing board, a non-slip mat to prevent her paper and books slipping when writing, a pair of scissors that can be used one-handed, a strap to maintain her sitting position, an adapted non-slip ruler and a tray that can be carried one-handed to move items from one position to another. Sally's teacher has established a buddy support system so that Sally is supported in group activities.	James needs support to read, write and produce independent work. He is dependent on the class teaching assistant to help him with many tasks, including transferring from one space to another. The school do have some resources to help James, but often fail to make these accessible.
Context	Sally is an only child and lives with her mum and dad in a small village. Her grandparents live nearby and are very supportive. Sally's father works in the local garden centre and her mum works part-time in her school as a dining assistant.	James is the youngest of four children, the survivor of twins. His parents are separated and he has limited contact with his father. His mother tries her hardest to make ends meet but often struggles with depression as a consequence of the family's financial difficulties.

A further case study has been provided for you to analyse at the end of this chapter.

The appreciation of the factors that are influencing the child's ability to learn can ensure that resources are allocated in the right direction. They highlight the fact that children with an identified medical or developmental condition do not have to be constrained by their diagnosis, and do not require labels to highlight their abilities and levels of need. In reality, the terms SA and SA+ replaced terms such an mild, moderate and severe learning difficulty, and had the purpose of identifying how many pupils teachers had to 'manage' in the typical classroom. This also led to the over-identification of SEN and distracted teachers away from their main priority of teaching pupils, assessing where they were in their learning and ensuring they got the right help where needed.

Unfortunately, the removal of these categories has also caused much anxiety, with teachers being challenged to address the unique individual learning needs of those pupils who may previously have received support under SA and SA+, including those who may have a 'statement' for their educational needs but **will not** qualify for a new education, health and care (EHC) plan.

It is therefore imperative that these pupils do not slip through the net and fail. The CoP recommends a **'graduated approach'** to meeting learning needs with a perpetual cycle of four actions being adopted:

1 **Assess.** The class teacher and SENCo should clearly analyse a pupil's needs before identifying a child as needing SEN support.

2 **Plan.** Parents must be notified whenever it is decided that a pupil is to be provided with SEN support.

3 **Do.** The class or subject teacher should remain responsible for working with the child on a daily basis. Where the interventions involve group or one-to-one teaching away from the main teacher, that teacher should still retain responsibility for the pupil.

4 Review. The effectiveness of the support should be reviewed on the agreed date.

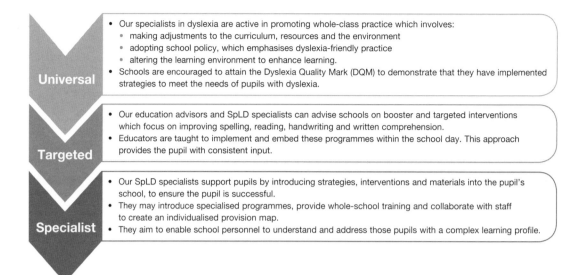

Support for pupils with dyslexia, courtesy of North Yorkshire County Council SpLD Service

There is no doubt that teachers will have to extend their knowledge of child development, in order to appreciate the links between:

O literacy and language development

O motor development, handwriting and PE

O sensory regulation and its impact on attention and behaviour.

If these associations are not recognised, we will see a downturn in positive outcomes. The focus on continuing professional development (CPD) should not focus on childhood conditions per se, rather the understanding of how they impact on the pupil's ability to learn.

Similarly, pupils with motor co-ordination difficulties, such as those seen in pupils with DCD, are also at risk if their teacher does not appreciate the impact of perceptual and motor differences on the pupil's performance, especially activities requiring handwriting, organisation and visual focus. This can lead to pupils' developing low confidence and becoming more vulnerable to being lonely and socially isolated (Bejerot, 2011). Sadly, there is evidence that these children have an increased risk of developing mental health difficulties due to poor self-esteem, and are more likely to be bullied (Campbell et al, 2012; Wilson et al, 2012).

Similar concerns are evident for pupils with more global learning difficulties. Given that approximately 19% of the population has a SEN or disability (DfE, 2013a), teachers will have to extend their expertise and ability to teach children and young people with a wide range of learning differences. A careful balance is therefore needed to appreciate the potential in a pupil who has divergent development.

The role of the **teaching assistant** (TA) has also been challenged in the revised legislation. There is no doubt that TAs play a crucial role in supporting the teacher to meet pupils' learning needs. However, in many instances, it is the TA who is playing the **lead role** in teaching the pupil with SEN. This has led parents to believe that it is only by obtaining funding for a TA, using hours of support as currency, that their child will receive adequate support in the classroom. In reality, too much reliance on TAs prevents pupils with SEN getting enough quality time with their teacher. Previously, battle lines were drawn in some parents' minds before they even approached the LA for support.

The CoP recommends a move away from the widespread default model of one-to-one TA support. It emphasises the significance of quality first teaching and gives a coded warning about how 'special education provision … is compromised by anything less' (Webster, 2014).

The Webster and Blatchford (2014) study of 48 primary school pupils with SEN who had statements showed they had a different educational experience to that of their non-SEN peers, characterised by fewer interactions with teachers and classmates, and almost constant and lower quality support from a TA. The study found that pupils with high level SEN receiving the most TA support made **significantly less academic progress** than similar pupils who received little or no TA support.

The CoP reinforces teachers' responsibility and accountability for the development and progress of all students in their class. The TA has a vital role in supporting the teacher in this. Webster (2014) rightly says that the key issue is that, from the very start, those working in the best interests of the child need to do more to help parents understand that the **quality** of support they receive really is more important than the **quantity**.

The new funding arrangements allow schools to be creative in using resources to either utilise TA support or purchase specialist input, such as speech and language therapy (SALT), teaching materials, resources and equipment. The school SENCo, together with the school leadership team, will need to demonstrate how the allocated funding can be used creatively to achieve positive outcomes with pupils who **do not** have an EHC plan. The continuing use of provision maps and inclusion passports should provide evidence of positive aspirations for all those pupils with additional learning needs. However, a future where every pupil has a personalised learning approach will see the demise of such profiles.

The ethos of the CoP focuses on functional and learning potential, with the premise that every child has learning differences that warrant personal teaching strategies.

Every teacher is responsible and accountable for all pupils in their class wherever or with whoever the pupils are working.
Children and Families Act, 2014

The argument about whether labels are necessary or not seem to always be a poor second to the human obsession for categorisation.
Boyle, 2013

If people with Down syndrome ruled the world
- Affection, hugging and caring for others would make a big comeback.
- All people would be encouraged to develop and use their gifts for helping others.
- People would be refreshingly honest and genuine.
- BIG dress up dances would flourish.
- People engaged in self-talk would be considered thoughtful and creative. Self-talk rooms would be reserved in offices and libraries to encourage this practice.
- Order and structure would rule.
- The words 'hurry' and 'fast' would be not be uttered in polite society. 'Plenty of time' would take their place.
- The most important news would be the weather, and remaining news would be local, i.e. 'A McDonald's has opened on…'

Dr Dennis McGuire, National Association for Down Syndrome

Group activity: Multi-faceted analysis of need (1)

Consider the following case study of a Matthew, aged 10, who is in a Year 6 class of a large urban primary school.

Matthew's family is sometimes confused by the involvement of a wide range of agencies and different professions.	Matthew lives with his parents and one-year-old sister. As his family have recently moved north, their friends and extended family are all in the south of England.	Mathew's ability to engage in play is limited by his lack of stability and voluntary movement.
Matthew is able to write the letters of the alphabet (albeit slowly).	Matthew is happy at school.	Matthew can read independently and loves reading.
Matthew is a bright, responsive child able to indicate his needs (non-verbally).	Matthew is a 10-year-old child with athetoid cerebral palsy with dystonic features.	Matthew can help to dress and undress himself.
Matthew can operate an expanded keyboard independently to type a short sentence.	Matthew struggles to pay attention when the class is noisy.	Matthew has a wicked sense of humour and often types rude jokes into his communication aid.
Matthew has some voluntary control of one arm and is able to assist with some activities such as eating and dressing.	Matthew is unable to access the PE changing rooms due to the narrow entrance.	Matthew is not able to walk or stand independently and has supported seating, a standing frame and a buggy.
Matthew has a new teacher with a limited understanding of physical disability.	Matthew has a TA who is with him throughout the school day.	Matthew would like to make friends but is restricted by his limited verbal skills.
Matthew uses a communication aid although his motor skills make this slow.	Matthew has a 'girlfriend' who travels in the taxi with him to school.	**Cut out each statement on this page.**

1 Place each statement in the appropriate sector on the Variable/influence mat on the following page.
2 Discuss your choices.
3 What are the implications of your choices on follow-up action?
4 What are the implications on funding?

Many of the answers are not set in stone and have been selected to promote debate among teachers and parents in order help identify the variables impacting on an individual's ability to learn. However, some guidance is provided on pages 98–99.

Group activity:
Multi-faceted analysis of need (2)

Variable/influence mat

Independent activity	Context

Body structure and functions	Environment

Personal factors	Participation

Implications for the leadership team

- School leaders will need to look at the current skill set of their staff, identifying gaps in abilities and ensuring relevant training and CPD.

- The role of the higher level teaching assistant (HLTA) and deployment of additional support should be appropriate. TAs should be under the direction of a teacher and be provided with training to meet the needs of the pupil they are deployed to support.

- Dedicated time must be planned to enhance quality first teaching methods.

- Rather than focusing on an overt childhood condition, such as foetal alcohol syndrome, for example, whole-school inset training should focus on linking development to learning profiles. For example, links between:
  - language and literacy
  - motor co-ordination and physical skills
  - the development of fine motor skills and handwriting
  - auditory development and attention
  - working memory and learning retention
  - perceptual development and cognition
  - sensory processing and engagement
  - comprehension and interpersonal communication.

- School leaders must regularly review how expertise and resources used to address SEN can be used to build the quality of whole-school provision as part of their approach to school improvement (CoP 6.3). Information can then be disseminated through the staff to enhance all teachers' skills, where necessary or appropriate. (NAHT, 2014).

- School leaders will need to be aware that Ofsted will expect to see evidence of pupil progress, a focus on outcomes and a rigorous approach to the monitoring and evaluation of any SEN support provided.

- School leaders need to set out a vision for the role and purpose of TAs in their school, defining the contribution they will make to learning. This means addressing some fundamental questions about what TAs can and should be expected to do, given that they tend not to have the same levels of teaching and subject knowledge as teachers.

Implications for SENCos

- SENCos will need sufficient time to focus on co-ordinating provision and ensuring that staff are skilled in delivering teaching and learning that is differentiated to the pupil's needs.

- SENCos will need to provide working examples to empower teachers to participate in the process of Assess, Plan, Do, Review.

- SENCos will need to analyse the variables that are impacting on the pupil's ability to learn and demonstrate how a graduated approach to meeting pupil need can be put into practice.

Implications for teachers

● The CoP encourages a dialogue between parents, carers, pupils and school staff in order to:

   ● set clear goals

   ● discuss the activities and support that will help achieve them

   ● review progress and identify the responsibilities of the parent, pupil and the school.

This can be a particular challenge in secondary schools where there pupils will have multiple teachers, there will be large pupil numbers and inconsistent communication systems.

● Teachers must take more responsibility for addressing the pupil's needs within the class, reducing the transfer of responsibilities to the SENCo, TA or external agencies. Indeed, the CoP stipulates that teaching staff are supported to manage these conversations as part of professional development.

● Teachers will be responsible for recording the provision made for pupils with SEN, and these should be kept up to date.

● Research has shown that teacher–TA liaison time before lessons is rare, so TAs often go into sessions without knowing what will be taught. TAs can only be as effective as teachers enable them to be, and should be informed of the skills or knowledge that the pupils they support should be developing, and what they need to achieve by the end of the lesson.

● Teachers need to show TAs how to scaffold skills for pupils, creating opportunities for pupils to practise and gradually fading out adult support.

Implications for governors

● The governors of maintained schools and academies have extended legal duties in relation to pupils with SEN, with particular emphasis on maintaining an awareness of the SEN provision within the school and supporting the implementation of SEN policy.

● Governors have a duty to share SEN information with parents of children who are planning to or who already attend the school.

● It is good practice for one governor to have a dedicated role in overseeing the provision for children and young people with SEN.

● Governors will need to be familiar with the reforms in SEN provision, paying particular attention to changes in the funding arrangements, as well as understanding the breakdown of the school's budget for SEN and how it is deployed.

CHAPTER 11
Further education

The Government has increased the age to which all young people in England must continue in education or training, requiring them to continue until the end of the academic year in which they turn 17 from 2013, and until their 18th birthday from 2015. The new legislation will give those young people with SEN aged 16–25 who wish to continue on to further education (FE) and training rights and protections comparable to those in school. However, it will require considerable collaboration between the pupil's school and a wide range of partner colleges to ensure that this transition is smooth and successful. It will involve liaison with local authorities (LAs) and services responsible for providing health and social care, and collaboration with training centres, employment agencies and housing associations to further the potential for the individual to become as independent and economically productive as possible.

Those young people who have previously had a statement for their learning needs, or Section 139a assessment (learning disability assessment (LDA)) will transfer to an education, health and care (EHC) plan, with appropriate support (and the financing of this) coming from education, health or social care providers. A period of time is being allowed to convert these plans; however, they must all be completed by 1 September 2016 if the young person is continuing in FE or training beyond that date.

The stipulations of the SEN Code of Practice (CoP) include regulations related to admissions to FE colleges and independent specialist providers (ISPs). The FE institution or ISP will now have a duty to admit the young person if it is named in their EHC plan.

If a young person's needs have not been identified during their school years, or should the young person experience a traumatic event which affects learning, then the FE college or ISP will be able to request an assessment of education, health and care needs from the LA, in a similar way to the school-based process. The FE colleges and ISPs are then required to engage with the LA and carry out annual reviews for students with EHC plans. These will need to focus on the young person's preparation for adulthood, employability, independent living and participation in society.

The CoP supports the key principles of **personalisation**, recommending that the young person is involved in making decisions about what they would like to do and how their needs can be met. This is the aspirational quality of the CoP, as previously the question 'What would you like to do?' would rarely be asked of many young people with SEN, particularly those with learning disabilities. Sadly, there was a legacy, in many institutions, of young people drifting from school to FE colleges or ISPs where the same courses were repeated year after year, leading to limited employment opportunities. It seems such as waste of resources that just 6.4% of young people with learning disabilities continue from college into paid employment and that approximately £330m a year is spent on FE for people with learning disabilities without this leading to the development of useful skills and productive employment. This is a waste of financial (and human) resources (Snell, 2011).

FE colleges and ISPs have the creativity to offer young people with SEN a wide range of qualifications covering many subjects. Courses include Entry Level 1, 2 and 3 Certificates and Awards, GCSEs, vocational GCSEs, AS and A Levels, National Vocational Qualifications and BTEC National Diplomas, Advanced Vocational Certificates and Special Diplomas. FE colleges and ISPs can also offer students the chance to take courses that help them develop skills such as independent living skills.

Most of these subjects can be made accessible, given the appropriate support, and assumptions should not be made that learners cannot do something because of a developmental difference or impairment. Deaf people can study music and students with dyslexia can train to be journalists (James, 2014).

The CoP places a renewed emphasis on ensuring that students leave college with adequate numeracy and literacy skills so that they can succeed in employment and/or independent living. This may require a different approach to that provided during the school years; after all, these young people will have previously received lessons in literacy and numeracy three or more times each week, for over ten years. In the FE college or ISP the focus may be on teaching alternative or compensatory strategies to ensure that life skills in literacy and numeracy are achieved. This may extend the use of a calculator or mathematical phone apps, talking books, voice-activated software, speech-to-text software, talking calculators etc.

Courses relating to literacy and numeracy are now mandatory, and institutions which do not offer maths and/or English courses to students aged 16 to 19 who have not yet achieved a GCSE grade C or above in those subjects will lose funding. This has had a bearing on the qualifications of FE teaching staff. This has been a controversial and political issue, as over the past year the Government has loosened the regulation that all lecturers and teachers in FE should have, or be working towards, a teaching qualification, in order to encourage the employment of staff with industrial expertise and skills. Although these regulations have not changed, the Government is boosting the expansion of workforce skills in this sector by providing promotional bursaries for high calibre graduates to undertake the specialist Diploma in Teaching Disabled Learners and become teachers in FE establishments (DfBIS, 2014).

When resources are scarce for everyone, people with learning disabilities tend to be overlooked or fall victim to a largely unspoken sense of 'why should "they" get anything?'
Snell, 2011

The new collaborative funding arrangements will require FE colleges and ISPs to forge closer links with LAs, who are the commissioners and funders of high needs students. However, the new funding arrangements will pose a positive challenge, as there are finances available to support internships, traineeships and apprenticeships, in partnership with employers.

FE colleges and ISPs would agree that the 'rights' stipulated in the CoP are legitimate and fair; however, there are real concerns regarding the ongoing resourcing of students who are not eligible for high needs funding; this is particularly a worry for specialist settings. It is important that this issue is addressed, so that positive outcomes become a reality.

The economic benefits of good FE training are considerable. Research by Kent Supported Employment, which helps people with disabilities who are looking for a job, found that for every person with a learning disability supported from FE college or ISP into work, there was an average saving for the council of £1,300 and £3,500 for the taxpayer (Kilsby & Beyer, 2011).

It is vital that this transition from FE college or ISP is managed well, at a time when market economics are biased towards the most capable. Interventions are required to ensure that school leavers have the skills, motivation and aptitude to compete on a level playing field with their peers. This may require the early introduction of key life skills typically introduced at 16+, to provide opportunities for those who may struggle with these to learn, and overlearn, strategies to enable them to fulfil their potential, be employable and contribute productively to society. In the long term, the FE college or ISP will need to support young people with SEN to find a job, explore further training opportunities, get involved in their local community, understand the services available to them as adults, find somewhere to live and explore the benefits they may be eligible for.

Finally, the FE college or ISP will be now be active in contributing to the local offer (LO), highlighting the courses and facilities available to young people with SEN. They will also be involved in contributing to local plans for the implementation of the reforms.

> *The new funding mechanism for SEN learners will mean there will be a cost-inspired race to the bottom as LAs seek to get FE to provide specialist support for less and less.*
>
> **Policy Consortium, 2014**

> *Don't tell me I can't, when I've already proven to so many that I can and have!*
>
> **Anon**

Implications for the leadership team

❶ FE/ISP leaders will have to develop closer links between the establishment and LA regarding the provisions made for young people with SEN.

❶ Planning will be required to help the young person in their transition into employment and independent living.

❶ FE/ISP leaders will be expected to contribute to the local plans for the implementation of the reforms.

❶ FE/ISP leaders will contribute to the development of the LO.

❶ Planning will be required to raise awareness of the reforms and organise workforce development to ensure that key staff become familiar with recommendations.

❶ FE/ISP leaders will also need to consider how the new funding and study programme arrangements can be used to tailor packages for young people with SEN, including supported internships, traineeships and apprenticeships, in partnership with employers.

❶ FE/ISP leaders must appreciate the positive changes in funding methods for post-16 students in schools and FE colleges.

❶ FE/ISP leaders can monitor whether there are comparable funding rates across settings.

Implications for SENCos/inclusion managers

● The SENCo or inclusion manager must adhere to recommendations within the CoP which now includes young people up to the age of 25 years.

● Learning difficulty assessments (LDAs) (and statements in schools) will be replaced by EHC assessments and plans, and SENCos/inclusion managers will be active in translating these into EHC plans.

● LDAs will be phased out by 31 August 2016 and therefore parents should be informed of these changes.

● Should a young person require an EHC plan, they must be actively involved in setting their own objectives. Families may still be involved in discussions but the young person can state how closely involved they would like their family to be; this decision should be respected. Until a young person is over compulsory school age (18+), parents or guardians have the final decision about their young person's plans.

Implications for teachers and tutors

● Teachers and tutors need to be aware of the changes in SEN reforms.

● Aspirational goals need to be established with each young person, leading to as productive and positive adulthood as possible.

Implications for governors

● The Government has outlined the new duties on FE colleges and ISPs from September 2014 including the following:

  ◉ The definition of SEN has been extended to include young people up to the age of 25; the definition includes 'learning difficulties' and 'disabilities'.

  ◉ FE colleges and ISPs will be required to 'have regard to' a new 0–25 SEN CoP.

  ◉ FE colleges and ISPs will have a duty to admit students if the institution is named in their EHC plan.

  ◉ FE colleges and ISPs, along with others, will be under a duty to co-operate with the LA to identify and meet the needs of young people with SEN.

CHAPTER 12
Preparation for adulthood

The transition from school into adulthood is, for many, an exciting time where the possibility to be more independent, and work or study towards a future career becomes a reality. Preparation for this is provided through opportunities to work part-time, increased personal independence and independent social interactions. This period can be more challenging for those with a SEN as the potential withdrawal of support provided throughout the school years can leave individuals and their families uncertain of what lies ahead.

Many young people with SEN need more time to prepare for adulthood, and the choices that their peers seem to make with apparent ease demand considerable more forward planning and extensive liaison between services in order to meet their needs. The transition from children's to adult services has, historically, been fraught with difficulties, with different funding systems, support mechanisms and even terminology, causing confusion and delay. For example, adult services for young people with severe learning disabilities come under the auspices of 'mental health'. This term can feel alien and inappropriate to families who have only experienced children's services.

In many instances, the differences between the two services previously caused a chasm which many families fell into, and although the principles of support were clear, the outworking could be patchy and inconsistent. Transitions between school, care settings and services are significant points at which people are particularly vulnerable to losing continuity in the support they receive. The expression 'standing on a cliff edge' was one frequently applied to this transitional process, with evidence that this results in young people and their families feeling insecure and anxious (Fegran et al, 2013). It is for this reason that the Children and Families Act 2014 recommends **early and extensive planning** which maintains the young person's desires and aspirations at the heart of the process.

The SEN Code of Practice (CoP) recommends that preparing for adulthood should start early and focus on four key areas:

Agatha Christie's dyslexia was so pervasive that she gave up on punctuation altogether, leaving her editor to deal with the petty details of full-stops and commas. She became the best-selling novelist of the 20th century.

Stevens, 2012

Professionals call it 'transitioning from high school'. Parents call it 'falling off the cliff'.

Nothing about us, without us.

1 further or higher education (FE/HE) and/or employment – this includes exploring different work/career options with help from the appropriate agencies.

2 independent living – this means young people having choice, freedom and control over their lives and the support they receive, their accommodation and living arrangements, including supported living

3 participating in society, including having friends and supportive relationships, and participating in, and contributing to, the local community

4 being as healthy as possible in adult life.

There are two aspects of transitioning to adulthood:

1 those transitioning to further or higher education (including ISPs) and/or employment

2 those who need continued support from social care and health services.

Young people have said that a good transition process depends more on support from practitioners than what transition model they receive.

Gordon, 2012

Transitioning to further or higher education and/or employment

The CoP recommends that transitional planning should start in Year 9 when young people are 13–14 years of age. The curriculum should encourage young people to think positively about their future. This is a challenging task at a time when most young people are struggling with the changes of puberty, of working out who they are and how they fit with an often unforgiving peer group. In addition, many schools have seen their careers services diminish, needing to be bought in when required, reducing the access to advice regarding future possibilities which was once available.

Special schools for young people with moderate or profound learning needs are well prepared in supporting their young people in the transition to adulthood, with a focus on life skills, independence, and self-care. However, preparation for students who attend mainstream provision can require more careful planning and consideration. The new CoP recommends that students should be encouraged to think about employment, independent living and community participation and that this should be developed through the curriculum and extra-curricular activities. However, there is a tension between the competing demands of a new educational curriculum (DfE, 2013d) and preparation for adulthood. Time is required to consider how this rhetoric can become a reality.

The following strategies can help pupils with SEN to participate in employment experiences in order to guide their decision process in establishing aspirational but realistic future goals.

Work experience

In most secondary schools, young people are given the opportunity to take part in work experience in Year 10. Approximately 95% of students in Key Stage 4 undertake work placements and about half of sixth form students have a further period of work experience or work-shadowing. These experiences give students first-hand knowledge of the skills required to perform a role and can be extremely effective in helping to identify the accommodations needed should the young person wish to pursue a career in this area (DfE, 2013d).

Students with SEN will require **more than one opportunity** to undertake work experience, in order to discover for themselves the dynamics of the working environment. This is particularly important for young people with autism for whom the description of what a job entails needs to be seen in the context of the working environment. For example, working as an IT programmer may seem to be the perfect career for a young person with Asperger's syndrome; however, the working environment may prove challenging, typically consisting of an open plan office with artificial lighting, shared with multiple computer users and telesales support responding to a consistent stream of noisy phone calls.

Workplace visits

These are beneficial to groups of students who may be interested in particular career or employment pathways. For example, time may be spent on a factory floor or in a laboratory.

Enterprise projects

The majority of secondary schools now have excellent links with local businesses. The opportunity to work with these employers can take the form of enterprise challenges. This is where the company set the students a brief to resolve a given problem or task within a specified timeframe. Alternatively, students can be involved in establishing a school-based enterprise, such as healthy break time snack bars, fund-raising initiatives, designing a phone app, etc. This activity encourages team working, leadership, good communication, working to deadlines, problem-solving and an understanding of business finance. Initiatives may also include visits to supermarkets to discuss pricing and stock turnover and to practise money management skills at the checkout.

Mentoring

This may involve employers in providing one-to-one encouragement and support to students who may be interested in pursuing an apprenticeship in a selected area, such as cookery skills for a student interested in becoming a chef.

Work shadowing

This gives students the opportunity to observe staff in real working environments, such as pharmacies, retail and therapy provision.

Employer workshops/talks

Schools regularly provide employer-led discussions with students about the realities of work and the employment and training environment. These can provide a forum in which specific questions can be asked which might be pertinent to those with a specific learning need.

Skills training

Some students require time to acquire skills that other students may routinely accomplish. For example, we know that young people with developmental co-ordination disorder (DCD) have difficulties learning to drive, with evidence that young adults with DCD make twice as many steering adjustments and are more reluctant than their peers to decelerate on time when driving down a straight course and negotiating a bend (deOliveira & Wann, 2011). This can be a disadvantage when at 17 their peers are succeeding in passing their driving test. Extra-curricular provision can help students to:

- access virtual driving simulators

- learn the Highway Code using apps such as the Hazard Perception Test

- learning to drive off-road in order to become familiar with handling a car. It is possible to do this from the age of 14 years.

For information about one provider see www.driveat15.com

Resilience modules

Many schools now incorporate modules which serve to enhance pupil resilience in the Year 10/11 curriculum. These are popular in the USA and serve to improve the confidence of potentially vulnerable learners, by incorporating activities which explore fairness, being in control, problem-solving, learning from mistakes, tolerance, forgiveness, assertiveness and relationships. In the UK, one particular resilience programme was trialled with Year 7 pupils attending 22 secondary schools. In a Government-sponsored project in 2010/11, short-term results were positive in improving students emotional wellbeing (DfE, 2011b). Sadly, recommendations to continue such programmes have been constrained due to the time required to implement the new National Curriculum and educational reforms.

Volunteering

Spending time volunteering can be a non-threatening way of exploring potential careers. For example, charity shops, care homes and nursery settings can often provide excellent opportunities for young people to explore their gifts and abilities, and this can help in future career-making decisions.

16–19 study programmes

The Government introduced a supported internships scheme to help young people aged 16 to 24 with complex learning difficulties or disabilities to find work (DfE, 2014c). These are primarily for students who have an education, health and care (EHC) plan. The scheme is mainly run by FE colleges with two aims:

1 to work with employers to find a job that suits the abilities of each intern
2 to create a unique study programme so all interns can learn the necessary skills to do the job.

These jobs are more likely to be in the fields of catering, retail and healthcare.

Many study programmes also provide students with the opportunity to study courses to develop other relevant skills, such as effective communication or understanding money.

Preparing for Adulthood (PfA)

Extensive support and guidance for young people with a disability and/or complex learning need in the transition to adulthood has been sponsored by Department for Education in partnership with the National Development Team for Inclusion, the Council for Disabled Children (CDC) and Helen Sanderson Associates. This partnership draws together expertise and experience in working with young people and families at a local and national level to support young people into adulthood, considering paid employment, good health, independent living and community inclusion. It recommends a personalised approach which keeps the individual's aspirations at the forefront of planning services. Influenced by this, several authorities have developed personalised learning pathways, creating a curriculum which leads to the achievement of selected outcomes. The creation of these plans requires LAs to collaborate with a variety of services including housing, adult and social care services.

Young people who need continued support from social care and health services

Continued support is given to all young people who are using children's health or social care services at the time when they are due to make a transition into adult health or social care services. This includes young people:

- O with mental health problems

- O who have disabilities, including physical and learning disabilities

- O with long-term, life-limiting and/or complex needs

- O in LA care.

> It will not include young people (aged up to 25) entering into adult health or social care services who were **not** previously using children's health or social care services.

This is supported by legislation in the form of the Children and Families Act 2014 **and** the Care Act 2014. The benefits of this collaboration are in pooling resources and funding, with the shared focus of aspirational and positive outcomes for young people. This will hopefully prevent young people and their families battling with systems to get the care and support required.

The following diagram shows the areas of agreement between legislation to support young people with complex physical and/or learning needs:

Children and Families Act 2014	Overlap in legislation	Care Act 2014
Overall ethos		
Outcomes-focused	✓	Outcomes-focused
Person-centred	✓	Person-centred
Children and young people engaged, empowered and supported to participate in planning for their future	✓	Aims to put people in control of their own care and support
Assessment		
Single, co-ordinated assessment process		Duty to carry out an assessment for young people over 18
Preparing for Adulthood outcomes from Year 9 (aged 13–14)		A child's needs assessment can be requested by young people or parents at any age; statutory duty to carry out a child's needs assessment if there are likely to be care and support needs post-18
Planning		
Preparation should encompass: • employment • health • independent living • friends, relationships • community participation	✓	Duty to promote wellbeing, should include: • control of day-to-day life (including the way care/support is provided) • participation in work, education, training or recreation • social and economic wellbeing • domestic, family and personal relationships • suitability of living accommodation • the individual's contribution to society

Children and Families Act 2014	Overlap in legislation	Care Act 2014
Integration		
Single EHC plan for young people with SEN, which can potentially continue up to the age of 25 years	✓	Duty to ensure integration of services across education, health and care, in particular where it promotes the wellbeing or improves the special educational provision that is available
Budgets and financial support		
Young people with an EHC plan may request a SEN personal budget	✓	Adult needs assessments carried out for individuals over the age of 18 years must include a personal budget
Right to request a direct payment	✓	Right to request a direct payment
Protecting the carer		
Duty to assess a parent-carer if it appears they may have need of support, or if they request an assessment, where the LA are satisfied that they may provide or arrange for the provision of services under Section 17 of the Children Act 1989. Must consider the extent to which the carer is participating in or wishes to participate in education, training or recreation, and works or wishes to work	✓	Duty to carry out carer's needs assessment where there is 'likely need' for support post-18 and when it is of 'significant benefit'. Carer's needs assessment must include an assessment of: • whether the carer is able, and is likely to continue to be able, to provide care and whether the carer is willing to do so • the outcomes that the carer wishes to achieve in day-to-day life. Whether, and if so to what extent, the provision of support could contribute to the achievement of those outcomes
Protecting young carers		
Young carers' needs assessment must have regard to the extent to which the young carer: • is participating in or wishes to participate in education, training or recreation • works or wishes to work	✓	Young carer's assessment must include an assessment of: • whether the carer is able, and is likely to continue to be able, to provide care and is willing to do so • the outcomes that the carer wishes to achieve in day-to-day life • whether, and if so to what extent, the provision of support could contribute to the achievement of those outcomes
Information		
Duty to develop a local offer of services and support available across education, health and care from 0–25 for disabled children and young people and those with SEN and their parents and carers		Duty to establish and maintain a service to provide information and advice relating to care and support for individuals and support for carers

Implications for the leadership team

● School and FE leaders must develop a shared vision for preparing for adulthood with young people, families and key stakeholders who work with young people aged 14–25.

● School and FE leaders must review the curriculum and programme modules and experiences which will prepare pupils for adulthood.

● School and FE leaders must develop a lifespan approach to establishing outcomes for pupils with SEN, ensuring that all professionals involved with the young person understand their role and responsibilities and how they relate to other stages of a young person's preparation for adulthood.

● School and FE leaders should develop capacity and competency in outcomes-focused support planning across children's and adult services.

● School and FE leaders must develop a process to allow the information from the EHC plan, including the CNA and personal budget holder's choices, to inform the joint commissioning strategy.

● School and FE leaders must provide extensive opportunities to prepare for the transition from school to FE/HE or employment, by programming activities which have an evidence base of success in this area into the school curriculum.

Implications for SENCos/inclusion managers

● When a young person receives, or is likely to receive, support from social care services, SENCos/inclusion managers must ensure that there is a representative from adult social care on the LA's SEN implementation board, so that plans put in place are agreed and embedded across service sectors.

● SENCos/inclusion managers must work with the young person to ensure that planning enhances and supports wider aspirations. These may relate to living in a shared home, independent living, employment hopes, skills for living, pursuit of certain leisure activities, relationships etc.

● In Year 9 SENCos/inclusion managers must ensure that pupils with SEN and their families receive information on how to request a CNA if they are likely to need care and support post-18.

● From Year 9, SENCos/inclusion managers should invite a relevant staff member from adult social services to be part of a pupil's transition review.

● SENCos/inclusion managers should engage teaching staff in understanding how to prepare students with complex needs for adulthood.

● SENCos/inclusion managers should discuss with the pupil and their family how to use personal budgets to enhance post-16 options and forms of support that lead to better outcomes for their future.

● SENCos/inclusion managers should work in collaboration with a relevant staff member from adult social services to indicate a personal budget for adult care and support.

Implications for teachers

● Teachers should personalise their approach for pupils with SEN, being aware of the goals they have established for their future.

● Teachers should raise aspirations for pupils with SEN by researching the achievements of those who have similar developmental differences or learning needs.

Implications for governors

● Governors should work with the school leadership team to schedule appropriate modules and experiences that will prepare pupils for adulthood.

● Governors should ensure that clear outcomes are in place for monitoring the effectiveness of PfA strategies.

● Governors should ensure there is a strategic approach to developing good informal advice and support for young people moving into adulthood.

CHAPTER 13
Education, health and care plans

The replacement of the statement of special educational needs and Section 139a learning difficulty assessment (LDA) with an education, health and care (EHC) plan that will run from birth to age 25 years is a radical and positive step in acknowledging the multiple variables that impact on an individual's ability to learn. It is also an excellent way of encouraging collaborative work to benefit the pupil. It acknowledges the influence of the home context on learning and makes health provision an accountable, integral part of the plan.

The plan will start by identifying the hopes and aspirations of the individual and their family. This will provide the basis from which interventions and support are allocated. This should lead to provisions based on personal need, rather than resources available. However, due to the new funding arrangements for SEN, the EHC plan will only be relevant to **a small percentage** of children and young people with highly complex physical and learning needs.

By placing the individual at the heart of the plan, and identifying the individual's unique skills, abilities and areas of need, provision will be innovative, personalised and based on evidence of what works. As such, the language of support will change, moving away from 'hours of entitlement' to 'resourcing' that meets outcomes. For example, a pupil who is struggling to physically record information may be allocated voice-activated software rather than a scribe; a pupil who is struggling with communication may be introduced to signing systems or a communication aid; and a pupil with limited mobility may request support from a team of peers rather than an adult assistant.

Therefore, the new plan will not stipulate hours of teaching assistant (TA) time, unless this targeted support has the intention of achieving a specific goal, such as a pupil needing support to undertake an intensive literacy intervention. Support from a TA in this scenario would be specific, time-limited and strive towards achieving a pre-determined goal.

This personalised approach places the responsibility for providing the pedagogic structure to achieve specified goals with the teacher. This will mean that the TA's role will be very different to those previously in place. The notion of the 'Velcro TA', attached to an individual pupil, will become rare, allowing pupils with SEN the opportunity to develop more meaningful relationships with their peers, which may have previously been constrained by the continual presence of a supportive adult.

In 2008, the Deployment and Impact of Support Staff (DISS) project found that those pupils who received most support from TAs made **less progress** in core subjects over a school year than similar pupils who received less support. This project emphasised that this was not the fault of individual

TAs, rather it reflected poor deployment of staff, a lack of preparation and differences in educational practice. For example, TAs were found to place greater stress on completing tasks rather than ensuring the pupil's learning or understanding.

The new reforms will signal a renewed impetus to enable TAs to fulfil the crucial role they have in facilitating the learning of the most educationally vulnerable pupils. They will have a very important role to play in helping to prepare materials for individuals with SEN, differentiating these according to the pupil's abilities. This should allow pupils to be fully included in their class, working on the same subjects as their peers, albeit at differing levels. The outcomes-focused nature of the Code of Practice (CoP) will require teachers to provide considerable guidance and forward planning to ensure that the right support and resources are in place to guarantee pupil progress.

Health provision

A further difference in the EHC plan is in health provision. Previously, health professionals could make recommendations to support the pupil's development and learning, but there was no legal accountability to provide this support. Now, the health service must co-operate with the LA in creating an EHC plan that stipulates the health provision that is reasonably required by the pupil. This could include specialist support and therapies, such as medical treatments and delivery of medications, occupational therapy to teach pupils with sensory processing differences self-regulatory strategies, or physiotherapy to maintain the mobility of a pupil with a degenerative condition such as muscular dystrophy, as well as a range of nursing support such as continence advice, specialist equipment and wheelchairs.

Health provision will be the responsibility of the commissioning body. This will normally be the local clinical commissioning group (CCG) but for children and young people with certain health conditions this may be NHS England. Health providers **must** engage with the LA to **jointly authorise arrangements** to meet the needs of pupils with SEN. These provisions need to set out what is required, why it is needed and who will be responsible for securing this. For example, physiotherapy input may be required to help the teacher and fellow pupils know how to assist a child with mobility difficulties to participate in PE lessons; or occupational therapy input to improve independent living skills prior to transition to a further or higher education (FE/HE) establishment.

Health professionals will have a shorter obligatory period in which to complete assessments which might support the EHC plan: 20 weeks rather than the previous 26 week framework. This may be a particular challenge to health professionals at a time when their own service is under financial review.

The long-term vision is that this collaborative planning will make efficiencies across SEN, specialist health and social care, through efficiencies such as reduced duplication of paperwork, context-based practice and collaborative goal-setting.

Social care provision

The social care provision specified in the EHC plan includes any resources or services that must be made for a child or young person under 18 by the LA as a result of Section 2 of the Chronically Sick and Disabled Persons Act 1970. This could include practical assistance in the home, home-based adaptations, short breaks (formerly termed 'respite') or family outings. It may also include adult social care provision for young people aged 18–25 with EHC plans.

The involvement of social services is vital in supporting the families of children with severe and complex needs, and new legislation now protects the health and emotional needs of primary carers. This involvement is crucial in ensuring the child or young person's wellbeing, which in turn will influence their capacity to learn. For example, disruptions in the night time regime will reduce the pupil's engagement at school.

The complexity and rapidly changing nature of children's needs and the diverse range of services that are often involved make integrated approaches particularly valuable. These ensure that families do not find themselves caught between different parts of the system, waiting for a particular service. The EHC plan offers an opportunity to ensure this does not happen. Therefore, the EHC plan has three fundamental attributes that can benefit pupils and their families:

1 There is more emphasis on gathering information from across services at the point of referral.

2 The family is much more involved through the co-ordinated assessment and planning stages.

3 It produces a plan which is more outcomes-focused and family-centred, having involved the people that matter: the child and his/her family (Spivak et al, 2014).

The differences between the statement and the EHC plan can be seen in the following table:

Statement	EHC plan
Completed within 26 weeks	Completed within 20 weeks
Previously divided into statement of need for 0–16-year-olds and learning disability assessments for 16–25-year-olds	One assessment for ages 0–25 years
Information gathered about the child/young person with an emphasis on professional opinions regarding the individual's needs. These reflected occupational bias	More person-centred with more engagement and involvement from parents, carers, children and young people in the process
Statutory assessment only considered the child or young person's educational needs	The EHC assessment must encompass education, health and care needs
Outcomes were professionally biased	Focuses on outcomes to be achieved for each child/young person
Parents/carers gave their views in writing and tended not to have opportunities for face-to-face meetings unless requested	Parents, carers, children and young people are actively involved in identifying their needs
The statement was written by a council officer (i.e. special educational needs officer (SENO)), schools were obliged to implement the plan and parents had the right to object	A more collaborative approach is envisaged with planning involving the child or young person where appropriate and their parent/carer
Recommendations often focused on hours of support (i.e. TA time)	Focuses on all the strategies which could enable the child/young person to learn (e.g. software, environmental adaptations, staff training)
No personal budgets attached to statement	Personal budget may be available to families to choose how to support the child or young person

The EHC planning pathway

Initial referral: requesting an EHC assessment (EHCAR)

The decision to initiate an EHC assessment will depend on the severity or complexity of a child or young person's needs and the steps previously taken to try to meet those needs, including how a setting, school or college has used its delegated budget and the resources available through the local offer (LO). An EHC plan will only be appropriate for a small percentage of children, young people and adults, who have highly complex needs.

The initial education, health and care assessment request (EHCAR) can be made by the school SENCo with the agreement of the pupil's parents, or directly by parents with the support of the child's setting. The request will only be accepted with the informed consent of the parent, carer or young adult. It can also be requested by a health professional, especially if the child has a complex developmental profile and attends the local child development centre for regular therapy.

Whoever initiates the request needs to provide their rationale for requesting an EHC assessment, together with considerable evidence to explain the child or young person's needs. Evidence could include a report from a speech and language therapist (SALT), educational or clinical psychologist, members of the Child and Adolescent Mental Health Services (CAMHS) team, to name but a few. In addition, families may ask that a new or different agency becomes involved with their child and the LA may pass this on as a request for service but cannot guarantee that the agency will agree to accept the referral.

The initial referral needs to describe the support that the child or young person may already be receiving and what progress has been made as a result of this. This support may have been accessed through services advertised in the LO.

Determining an EHC assessment

On receipt of this request for an assessment, the LA will have six weeks to review the details provided and either accept or reject the request on the basis of the information provided. This will be the responsibility of a minimum of two designated officers.

If the request for an assessment is rejected, the LA must indicate why, and direct the individual to support available through the LO. Individuals will be informed how to appeal against this decision if they feel it is unfair.

If the request for an assessment is accepted, the LA must inform the individual and their family. However, they must also explain that the assessment **may not** lead to the provision of an EHC plan, as the LA may indicate ways in which the school, college or other provider can meet the child or young person's needs without this. The LA must immediately inform all services involved with the child or young person that this assessment is going ahead. This will include relevant colleagues in health, social services and education, or other service providers such as youth justice.

The EHC assessment process

The assessment process will be person-centred, and will gather and collate any further information about the goals and aspirations of the child or young person and their family. This process should not require the family to repeat information, rather add to the procedure. The will provide an indication of which outcomes the family would like the provision to address. In collating this information, the

LA must ensure that parents and young people have been fully consulted and have been given the opportunity to share their views and to submit any additional evidence, if they wish to.

Initial questions may be asked:

- O What is going well/not going so well for the young person?
- O What is important to the young person now and for the future?

The LA panel will look at the gathered information and evidence provided across education, health and social care to obtain a holistic understanding of individual needs at this point. Further information may be sought from other agencies before agreeing that an EHC plan is necessary. The information provided should reflect what has already been tried and, in a school or college setting, should describe how the notional SEN funding has been used.

The panel will then consider the outcomes that the individual would like to achieve. These might include the following examples:

- To support the development of attention and concentration

- To support the development of speech and communication; so that his receptive understanding of language and his expressive use of language are functional and in line with the rest of his development

- To make and maintain friendships.

EHC plan example, DfE, 2014d

Various templates are being used to frame the assessment, most include the following sections:

- O My family history
- O My family's one-page profile
- O My one-page profile
- O How to support me
- O My support plan
- O Review sheet (outcomes and provision).

Approving the plan

The decision about whether a plan is required or not must be made within 16 weeks of receipt of the first request. If the plan is considered to be the most appropriate way forward in helping the individual achieve their goals, the LA will convene a person-centred planning meeting, or team-around-the child (TAC) meeting, which will involve the child or young person, their parents/carers, the lead professional/key working partner and key health, education and social care professionals. Together they will analyse the outcomes requested and discuss how these may be achieved. They will then agree a budget to support the agreed provision and establish a date when progress will be reviewed.

The plan will be clearly structured, identifying the outcomes the individual would like to achieve. Each outcome will be SMART:

- **S**pecific
- **M**easurable
- **A**chievable
- **R**ealistic
- **T**ime-bound.

Funding will be discussed and the family will be informed about the possibility of holding a personal budget or letting the LA arrange the details on behalf of the individual and their family. Funding may come from multiple sources and these must be agreed at this meeting.

Throughout the EHC plan journey, opportunities for mediation will be made explicit, especially when a plan or budget is not agreed. The whole journey must take 20 weeks from start to finish, unless particular circumstances prevail. Details relating to this plan, together with examples of evidence, outcomes and resources are provided within the CoP.

Implications for the leadership team

- Senior school leaders must appreciate the EHC plan process and their responsibility in providing detailed information regarding pupil progress.

- New relationships with colleagues in health, social care and other agencies external to the school will require school leaders to clarify roles and responsibilities and manage schedules relating to these providers.

- For those pupils who may have missed out on receiving an EHC plan, following the assessment, some LAs are recommending a 'mini plan' which can be actively supported by the school.

- School leaders need to familiarise themselves with the Special Educational Needs (Personal Budgets) Regulations 2014 to respond to requests by parents who may have been allocated a personal budget to meet an educational outcome as part of their child's EHC plan.

- The headteacher, principal or equivalent will be responsible for giving written consent to the LA for receiving direct payments for any goods or services which are to be used or provided in a school or post-16 institution.

- School leaders will have to ensure SENCos have adequate time to convert qualifying pupils' statements to EHC plans.

Implications for SENCos

- SENCos must carefully collate information regarding the progress of pupils with complex needs. This must be clearly evidenced in the event of an EHC request being made.

- SENCos should make sure reports from external professionals or educational psychologist (if available) are held with the pupil's records.

- If the SENCo believes that the pupil may benefit from an EHC plan they must liaise with the pupil and their family, discussing the rationale for doing this, prior to making the request for an EHCAR.

- If a pupil's family wish to submit an EHCAR, the SENCo must guide them on the appropriateness of this, and advise whether the pupil's needs could be better met by services identified in the LO.

- SENCos will be active in converting information from a pupil who has a statement for their SEN to an EHC plan.

Implications for teachers

- Teachers need to carefully monitor pupils' performance, establishing specific goals with measurable outcomes for those who appear to be struggling.

- Teachers may have to provide evidence regarding educational provision and pupil progress to the LA should a parent or other relevant agency request an EHCAR.

- Teachers should consider recording information which reflects more qualitative aspects of the pupils performance, such as attention span, behaviour, outbursts, engagement etc.

Implications for governors

- Governors need to become familiar with the following regulations to ensure that the school is accountable in enabling a pupil to achieve the outcomes stipulated within an EHC plan:
  - The Special Educational Needs and Disability Regulations 2014
  - The Special Educational Needs (Personal Budgets) Regulations 2014
  - The Community Care Services for Carers and Children's Services (Direct Payments) Regulations (DH, 2009)
  - The National Health Service (Direct Payments) Regulations 2013.

CHAPTER 14
Children and young people in specific circumstances

The SEN Code of Practice (CoP) (2014) considers children and young people in specific circumstances who may need **additional** consideration under the Children and Families Act 2014. This includes children and young people who:

- are looked after (i.e. 'in care')
- are care leavers
- have SEN and social care needs, including children in need
- are being educated out of area
- have SEN and are educated at home
- are in alternative provision
- have SEN and are in hospital
- are in youth custody
- are children of service personnel.

The facets of the CoP described in previous chapters are applicable to all these children and young people; therefore this chapter will highlight features which are pertinent to selected groups whose circumstances may influence their education.

Looked-after children

There are over 92,000 looked-after children in the UK. Around 70% of these have some form of SEN, with approximately 50% having emotional and health needs which may provide their teachers with a challenge. Unfortunately, the vulnerable start in life and pre-care experiences of these children can result in the late identification of learning needs. This is mainly due to two reasons.

Firstly, some of the symptomatic behaviour of additional learning needs, such as defiance, withdrawal or outburst, might be assumed to be only a result of poor pre-care experiences.

Secondly, frequent moves between care settings, carers, schools and social workers mean that establishing a secure and stable home environment rightly takes precedence over educational goals. This is a major concern, as on average only 17% of all fostered children aged between five and 18 stay in the same placement for more than five years. This implies that the majority of children have multiple placements impacting on their stability, security and subsequent education (DfE, 2013c).

> During 2011–12, 43% of children who had had a single care placement achieved 5+ A*–C grades at GCSE. Only 13% of those who had experienced three or more placements achieved the same result.

To limit the effect of the insecurity and instability issues faced by the majority of looked-after children, legislation has recommended that each LA has a virtual school team, led by a virtual school head (VSH), who can provide consistent support and carefully track the progress of children **as if** they attended a single school.

Members of the virtual school team will liaise closely with the school's designated teacher (DT) for looked-after children to realise the pupil's outcomes. The DT, a member of the virtual school team and the school SENCO will work closely together to ensure that the implications of a child being both looked after **and** having SEN are fully understood by relevant school staff.

Extra funding has been allocated to support looked-after children and from April 2014 there will be a pupil premium plus for looked-after children of £1,900 per child per year; this is double the previous grant! This grant will be managed by the VSH rather than the child's school, to avoid the administrative challenges involved should the child need to move schools. It will now be available from the first day the child enters care, and can be used to pay for a range of services, such as one-to-one booster sessions, speech and language therapy support or musical instrument lessons. This grant is also available to children who have been adopted.

The responsibility for assessing and funding an education, health and care (EHC) plan will continue to be the responsibility of the LA in which the pupil normally resides. This may be different from where the child or young person attends school. These children will often also have a care plan, a personal education plan and a health plan, and therefore the virtual school team must work with the school, social worker and foster family/adoptive family/care setting to ensure that the EHC plan is in harmony with these other plans.

Pupil premium linked to children in special circumstances	Pupil premium per child
Disadvantaged pupils	
Pupils in Years R to 6 recorded as free school meals (FSM) Ever 6*	£1,300
Pupils in Years 7 to 11 recorded as FSM Ever 6	£935
Looked-after children	£1,900
Children adopted from care under the Adoption and Children Act 2002 and children who have left care under a special guardianship or residence order	£1,900
Service children	
Pupils in Years R to 11 recorded as Ever 4 Service Child** or in receipt of a child pension from the Ministry of Defence	£300

Pupil premium linked to those with special circumstances 2014/2015 (DfE, 2014a)

* Ever 6 FSM refers to those pupils recorded on the January 2013 School Census who were recorded as known to be eligible for free school meals (FSM) on any of the termly censuses since summer 2007, including the January 2013 School Census.

** Ever 4 Service Child means a pupil recorded on the January 2014 census who was eligible for the Service Child premium in 2011–12, 2012–13 or 2013–14, as well as those recorded as a Service Child for the first time on the January 2014 School Census.

Care leavers

Prior to the introduction of the Children and Families Act 2014, legislation relating to young people in care ceased to apply when they turned 18. This affected those who would have benefitted from support and security in the transition to further or higher education (FE/HE), apprenticeships or employment. The new legislation has stipulated that LAs must now establish 'staying put' arrangements so that young people can gain this support until they are 21 years old.

The terminology used to describe these young people reflects a different type of support, in that the individual is termed a young adult and a care leaver; as such they are entitled to the support of a personal adviser employed by the LA. The personal adviser will guide the young person in developing a pathway plan (PP). The PP plots transition from care to adulthood for care leavers up to the age of 25 years, if they remain in education and/or training or are not in employment, education or training and plan to return to education and/or training.

Children and young people with SEN and social care needs

Some children and young people with SEN are particularly vulnerable and require the support of social care. The involvement of social care services will be determined by the level of risk and whether the individual is perceived to be vulnerable to harm. Some pupils with significant learning needs may have parents who are also vulnerable and require ongoing support in parenting a child with SEN. The document Working Together to Safeguard Children 2013 (DFE, 2013e) is particularly relevant to these children and young people. In situations where an individual's needs warrant a care plan, their social worker will be actively involved in EHC plan reviews, which should ideally be synchronised with social care plan reviews, and once again, must **always** meet the needs of the individual child or young person.

Children and young people educated out of area

Where a child or young person being educated out of an LA's area is brought to their attention as potentially having SEN, the **home** LA (where the child normally lives) should decide whether to assess the child or young person and whether an EHC plan is required. This LA will be obliged to fund any recommendations. This will not include private school fees unless the out-of-county school is a specialist provider.

Children and young people in alternative provision

The SEN reforms are applicable in their entirety to pupils educated in provisions such as pupil referral units (PRUs), specialist units or free schools.

Children of service personnel

Children of service personnel may face unique difficulties. These needs may arise from:

- service induced mobility. Service personnel may relocate more often than the rest of the population and sometimes at short notice. Such transitions should be well managed to avoid service children with SEN experiencing delays in having their needs assessed and met

○ the deployment of serving parents to operational arenas, while not constituting SEN in itself, may result in a service child experiencing anxiety, dips in educational performance and/or emotional difficulties. Children may also be affected similarly by the deployment of siblings

○ family **relationship problems** on return from deployment

○ potential **exposure** to toxic/chemical substances.

> *There has to be some way of service children having a SEN passport of some sort that can move from LA to LA and at least give the new school a starting point.*
> **MOD, 2013**

The biggest concern for pupils in this category is the smooth transfer of information about the child between different schools, which may be in the UK or overseas. To address this, the Ministry of Defence (MOD) has developed the pupil information profile for service children, which includes details of a child's SEN. It is available for use by schools across the UK and overseas and is available from the Children's Education Advisory Service (CEAS). CEAS is an integral part of Directorate Children and Young People (DCYP), which is the focal point within the Ministry of Defence for all matters relating to service children and young people. This organisation can also help in providing funding so that the child or young person with SEN can reside in a special school which meets their needs.

For most pupils, the local offer (LO) will provide information regarding services to support their needs. However, this is more problematic for mobile service families as the LO will differ from LA to LA and also from England and Wales to Scotland. The House of Commons Defence Committee is seeking to address these difficulties through the Armed Forces Covenant in Action (2013). This encourages LAs to seek advice from CEAS, acting on behalf of the Secretary of State for Defence, when creating EHC plans, and in certain situations extra funding in the form of a special educational needs addition (SENA) allowance may be available, if the family are in receipt of a continuity of education allowance (CEA), financial support which addresses the effect on mobility on service children and families.

Implications for the leadership team

❶ School leaders need to be aware that financial support is available to assist children and young people in special circumstances.

❶ Staff may need continuing professional development (CPD) to enhance their understanding of children in special circumstances, particularly those with social, emotional and mental health needs.

Implications for SENCos

- SENCos must develop a working relationship with members of the virtual school team if there are looked-after children on their roll.

- Children who are looked after will need their levels of ability monitored from school entry with early intervention or booster sessions provided to optimise learning opportunities.

- SENCos must contribute to the pupil information profile of children with SEN who are from a service family.

- SENCos may find it important to develop a working relationship with the child's social worker so that home–school liaison is effective.

Implications for teachers

- Teachers need to appreciate the unique difficulties faced by children in special circumstances but must not use these as an excuse for limited development.

- Teachers should ensure that aspirations remain high despite difficult circumstances.

Implications for governors

- Governors will have a role in making sure schools are accountable for the use of their pupil premium and pupil premium plus grants, ensuring that this money is used to raise outcomes.

- Governors will contibute to putting measures in place to ensure that grants are successfully used to improve individual outcomes.

CHAPTER 15
SEN funding reforms

The funding arrangements for schools were changed in April 2013 to reflect the new legislation and ways of working. In the past, schools were allocated various amounts by their local authority (LA) based on a number of complex formulae. The reform now gives a sum of money **directly** to schools, making it possible for them to make their own decisions as to how to support pupils with a range of needs. The funding changes have not, however, changed the legal responsibilities of schools and LAs for those with SEN.

> Although academies are funded through the Education Funding Agency they will also get the same level of funding for each pupil as LA schools in their area.

The new reforms were intended to be fairer and mean that funding is agreed locally and given to schools under three main headings:

1 Core education funding. This is an amount of money allocated for each pupil in the school.
2 Additional support funding. This is the school's **notional SEN budget**.
3 Top-up funding, also known as individually assigned resources (IAR).

Core education funding

Schools get most of their annual funding based on the total number of pupils in the school. Every pupil in a school attracts an amount of money. The amount varies from one LA to another. This is primarily due to location (property prices and salaries are higher in London) or deprivation (low income households). In addition, there is usually more core funding per pupil in a secondary school than in a primary school. In 2013, all secondary schools, including academies, were getting at least £3,000 per pupil per year and all primary schools were getting at least £2,000 per pupil per year. This is the **core budget** for each school and it is used to make **general provision** for all pupils in the school, including pupils with SEN.

Additional support funding

Every school receives an additional amount of money to help make special educational provision to improve the attainment of those with additional learning needs. This is called the **notional SEN budget**.

The amount of money allocated in this way is based on a formula agreed between schools and the LA. The formula usually gives more money to schools that have more children on free school meals (FSM) and the deprivation index, and more pupils who are not doing as well as others in English and maths. This provides a good guide as to how many pupils with SEN a school is likely to have because there is a high correlation between these factors and learning difficulties.

A small number of schools may find they have many more pupils with SEN than expected but are eligible for less money due to lower deprivation factors. This might happen where, for example, a school has a good reputation for teaching pupils with SEN and so attracts additional pupils. Where this does happen, the school can ask the LA for additional funding.

The Government has recommended that schools should use this notional SEN budget to pay for **up to £6,000** worth of special educational provision to meet a pupil's individualised need. Most pupils with SEN need special educational provision that costs less than £6,000 per year. Schools need to be accountable and explain clearly how they have used this money, what they have provided, for how long and how effective it was. The term 'notional' is used because the school have the freedom to decide how it is used. This budget can be used for anything that is 'additional to or different from' the provision that is made for all pupils, such as specialised technology, learning equipment or software, time with a specialist teacher or speech and language therapy (SALT) input.

Top-up funding/IAR

If the school can show that a pupil with SEN needs more than £6,000 worth of special educational provision, it can ask the LA to provide top-up funding to meet the cost of that provision. This can be requested with or without an education, health and care (EHC) plan; however, there needs to be a clear explanation as to why this money is required and what it will be used for.

If your school says they do not have enough funding to meet the first £6,000 for all the children with SEN at the school: ask the school whether it has approached the local authority for additional SEN funding.

Council for Disabled Children, 2013

High needs funding will usually cover placement in:

- special schools
- special units
- mainstream schools and academies for pupils with high needs
- alternative provision, that is pupil referral units (PRUs)
- post-16 institutions: further education (FE), schools and other providers
- independent non-maintained special schools (INMSS).

| | | Pre-16 SEN and AP | | Post-16 SEN and LDD |
		Mainstream settings	Specialist settings	All settings
Element 1: Core education funding		Mainstream per-pupil funding (AWPU)	Base funding of £10,000 for SEN and £8,000 for AP placements, which is roughly equivalent to the level up to which a mainstream provider would have contributed to the additional support provision of a high needs pupil. Base funding is provided on the basis of planned places	Mainstream per-student funding (as calculated by the national 16–19 funding system)
Element 2: Additional support funding		Contribution of £6,000 to additional support required by a pupil with high needs, from the notional SEN budget		Contribution of £6,000 to additional support required by a student with high needs
Element 3: Top-up funding		"Top-up" funding from the commissioner to meet the needs of each pupil or student placed in the institution		

Overview: reform of high needs funding, DfE, 2012

This high level funding will be used to resource provisions required to help pupils with SEN achieve their outcomes. These will be time-limited and carefully evaluated to ensure that the pupil is meeting their objectives. For example, this funding could pay for input from a speech and language therapist to improve expressive language or pay for voice-activated software to improve written communication.

From 2014 parents may request that aspects of this high level budget are given to them in the form of a **personal budget** to enable them to provide the resources needed to help their child or young person achieve their desired outcomes.

Personalised budgets and direct payments

Personal care budget

Personalised budgets have been available in **social care** settings since 2008 and were introduced to meet the 'personalisation agenda'. The Community Care (Direct Payments) Act 1996 gave LAs the power to allocate money in lieu of services to a disabled person who met their eligibility criteria and who preferred this arrangement. This law was the result of many years of campaigning by people with disabilities, who argued that they would have greater choice and control if they had a cash payment rather than a standard service. Therefore, following a needs assessment a sum of money was allocated to provide a package of services which helped individuals to live as independently as possible in their own community. The package of support enabled individuals to buy their own care, or the care for a child with a complex physical and/or learning need.

These packages of support are available to:

O a parent, or other person with parental responsibility for a child with a disability, and persons with a disability with parental responsibility for a child

O young people aged 16 and over with a disability, for their own needs

O people whom the council decides need services because they provide or intend to provide a substantial amount of care on a regular basis for someone aged 18 or over

O an appointed 'suitable person' to organise support on behalf of someone lacking the mental capacity to do it themselves (Gheera, 2012).

Personal health budget

In keeping with the personalisation agenda, a **personal health budget** scheme was trialled in 2012 with money from the National Health Service (NHS). This helped individuals with an identified **health need** to buy services which would improve their health and wellbeing. This budget could be used to buy therapies, personal care, respite care, equipment and self-management courses. Personal health budgets focus on what people want to achieve in the future, rather than on what services the NHS has previously provided. This is based on evidence that when people are actively engaged in decisions about their health and wellbeing, their outcomes are significantly improved. In line with SEN reforms, children who were previously eligible for support through continuing care will be able to have the health provision of their support provided as part of an EHC plan.

NHS England provides the following example of how a personal health budget can be used.

Tory

Case study: Dan

Dan has cerebral palsy. He needs regular physiotherapy, but sometimes is unable to access it on the NHS for long periods. This leaves Dan in pain, with severe postural problems. With his personal health budget Dan can access weekly physiotherapy, seeing improvements in his muscle control, posture, speech and breathing. Through the care planning process, equipment was also identified that will help Dan manage his condition better. Now Dan can communicate more clearly and lead a full and active life, including attending college and pursuing his passion for music.

Personal SEN budget

The apparent success of the provision of personalised budgets for health and social care has encouraged the Government to recommend a similar plan for children to help meet their educational aspirations. This is known as the **personal SEN budget** and is focused on learning outcomes. Money will come from the top-up funding/IAR described on pages 89–90 depending on need; however, this funding **will not** be available to all children and young people with an EHC plan.

This budget can be used to provide any additional individual support the child or young person needs in order to achieve the learning outcomes set out in their EHC plan or statement of SEN. Budgets will only be approved by the health, education and social care authorities when a clear and sensible set of outcomes is agreed. **Parts** of the personal SEN budget may be taken as a direct payment and used by parents on behalf of the pupil to purchase the additional and individual support set out in the EHC plan (e.g. any assessed support which is **not** already provided by the school). Families **do not** have to accept this offer: if they prefer they can still receive support in the traditional way, which means that services will be organised for them.

There are four ways in which the personal budget can be managed. The family can:

1 choose to take the personal budget as a direct payment and manage it themselves (with options available for support to do this)

2 ask a third party service or organisation to manage it on their behalf; this is often called an individual service fund (ISF)

3 ask the LA to manage it on their behalf

4 choose to have a mix of the three options: part-direct payment, part-ISF and part-managed by the LA.

> In some circumstances, the option to take a personal budget as a direct payment may be withheld. This is likely to be a result of concerns around safeguarding and/or consent (in particular for 16- and 17-year-olds).

The availability and distribution of a personalised budget has raised some anxieties for schools, with concerns being raised that parents may want to employ their own teaching assistant (TA) in their child's class or spend their budget on resources and interventions which have a spurious evidence base for success. This will be monitored by the team-around-the-child when EHC outcomes are established.

Personal (collective) budget

The ultimate goal of the EHC plan is to draw together children and families with professionals in health, social care and education to provide one personal budget which will support the child or young person in all aspects of life. This will require extensive collaboration, joint commissioning and collective planning. Joining up these three funding streams – social care, health and education – will be a very real challenge for the authorities, given that the funds are provided for quite different purposes and channelled through very different routes. However, the outcome will hopefully be very positive. The driving force behind personal budgets is the **person-centred planning process**.

According to In Control, the advantages of this combined budgeting approach to meeting the needs of children and young people with high needs are:

○ transparency: everyone understands what is happening and when and how decisions are reached

○ participation: everyone who needs to take part can do so, and those who need support to participate are supported to do so.

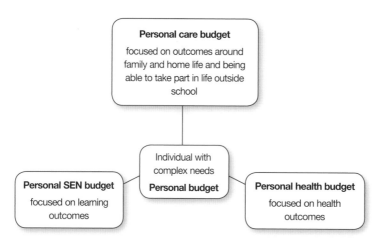

Personalised budgets

Consider how the combined budgeting approach could be applied to this hypothetical case study:

Case study: Carrie

Carrie is 8 and has Niemann–Pick type C. This is a progressive (degenerative) neurological disease and is responsible for gradual physical deterioration, learning disability and premature death. Carrie lives with her mum and younger brother and sister in a housing association property. Carrie's mum is totally responsible for her care and has struggled lately as she has strained her back.

Carrie attends a local special school. She has limited independent movement, although she can operate an electric wheelchair with her thumb and index finger. She is non-verbal, but can 'communicate' her wants and needs using her eyes to identify a direction or respond to questions. She cannot feed herself and is enterally fed during the evening.

Carrie enjoys being with others. She loves music and is passionate about her favourite band; she plays their music as often, and as loud, as she can. She is unaware that she may not live into adulthood but would like to be as independent as possible for as long as she is able.

Carrie's mum highlights the aspirations for her daughter and the rest of the family as follows:

- Carrie's mum requires help in meeting Carrie's self-care needs, especially bathing due to concerns over her 'dodgy' back.
- Carrie would like a method of communication which would enhance her interactions with others.
- Carrie would like to be less reliant on others within her home.
- Carrie would like an opportunity to join in an after-school music group.
- Carrie's mum would like some short break support (especially during school holidays) so that she can give her younger children more one-to-one time.

The pooling of resources from health, social care and education sectors could enable Carrie and her family to achieve their desired objectives.

Personal health budget	Personal social budget	Personal SEN budget
Specialised electronic adjustable bed	Short break support for 5–8 hours each week	Eye-gaze technology switch to operate computer
Ripple mattress to aid circulation	Hospice break	Blink-controlled switch operation to use with computer
Electronic hoist to aid transfers into and out of the bath	Personal carer to help with self-care activities	Speech and language therapist to help Carrie use her communication aid
Support for continence care at home and school	Steeper or possum environmental control system	
	Air-responsive door-opening devices	

Funding is reviewed annually and may change if:

- the child's needs have changed
- the child has reached their learning targets
- new methods have been introduced that meet the child's needs.

There are many **positive** aspects to these funding changes:

- Pupils in mainstream schools will receive equal funding to those in specialist provision with similar needs.
- There is a partial return to the principle that 'the money will follow the child'.
- There is accountability in SEN expenditure.
- Schools will be able to spend the delegated SEN budget across all children with SEN. (This could fund equipment or a specialist teacher to support many pupils.)
- Schools are now given more funding for SEN as part of their school budget.
- Headteachers, principals and governors can see more clearly how their budgets have been set and can plan more effectively, responding to demand from parents.

- ○ The simplified local formulae will reduce the administrative burdens on maintained schools, academies and the Education Funding Agency as the process will be much simpler.

- ○ The focus will be on providing creative means to improve individual attainment rather than hours of teaching/TA support.

However, there remain many **concerns** around these changes:

- ○ Schools may still argue that their delegated SEN budgets are insufficient, particularly if they have a large number of high needs pupils on roll.

- ○ Small schools may struggle financially.

- ○ It will take time to change perceptions that funding can be used on more than staffing support.

- ○ Parents or carers may struggle to accept changes in provision, especially if their child has received TA support for a prolonged period.

The key ingredient to living independently was my personal budget. I am now living as independently as I can, in my own place on an ordinary street with my own personal assistants helping me with my day to day life. I was able to be fully involved in all the planning and interviewed my own personal assistants. They are the same type of age as me and I get on with really well with them.

In Control, 2014

Implications for the leadership team

- ❶ School leaders must demonstrate what they are providing for pupils with SEN, how much this costs and whether it achieves positive outcomes.

- ❶ Schools that require access to top-up funding must provide their LA with clear evidence that the input provided has enabled pupils to progress.

- ❶ Details regarding how funding has been used to meet pupil outcomes must be published in the school SEN LO.

- ❶ School leaders must provide CPD to ensure that all staff understand funding changes and the implications to the school.

- ❶ School leaders must ensure that the SENCo has administrative time to respond to changes in SEN provision.

Implications for SENCos

- ❶ SENCos will be responsible for establishing collaborative outcomes with the pupil and their family, ensuring that these are SMART.

- ❶ SENCos will need to account for the provisions and resources which have been allocated to enable the pupil to achieve these goals.

Implications for teachers

- Teachers will be more accountable for the progress of pupils with SEN, even those who receive extra support from specialist staff.

- Teachers should expect to be judged in their appraisals on how well they teach pupils with SEN.

- Teachers will have to use additional adults effectively to ensure progress.

Implications for governors

- Governors need to monitor how many pupils in the school have SEN and how much money the school receives to support them in order to ensure the appropriate allocation of funds.

- Governors must ensure that the provisions specified in statements of SEN and EHC plans are made.

- Governors must ensure that SEN provision is integrated into the school improvement plan.

ANSWERS

Quiz: How far have we come? (page 10)

Eugenics Education Society 1907; The Mental Deficiency Act 1913;
The Education Act (following Norwood Report) 1944; Education (Handicapped) Act 1970;
Warnock Report 1978; Disability Discrimination Act 1995; National Curriculum 1988;
Special Educational Needs & Disability Act (SENDA) 2001; Every Child Matters 2003;
Removing Barriers to Achievement 2004; Rose Review of Literacy 2006; Lamb Enquiry 2009;
Equality Act 2010; Support and Aspiration: A new approach to special needs and disability 2011;
Children and Family Act 2014.

Quiz: Equality Act (pages 17–18)

1 c; **2** b; **3** b; **4** c; **5** c; **6** a; **7** a; **8** true; **9** c; **10** b; **11** false; **12** d; **13** b; **14** no; **15** true; **16** true.

Activity: Working together (pages 34–36)

Education	Health	Social care
The class TA may join the social skills group run by the speech and language therapist (SALT) so that the strategies introduced are encouraged throughout the school day. The SENCo will be responsible for monitoring and reviewing learning outcomes. The SENCo will also be involved in writing Chloe's inclusion passport. The teacher will actively differentiate learning material so that Chloe can attempt this with minimal support. The headteacher may review classroom lighting to reduce the negative effects on Chloe's vision and attention. A specialist teacher of autism can be invited to run an autism awareness session to deter pupils from teasing Chloe. A similar twilight session can be held to enable school staff to understand her needs. A specialist literacy advisor may recommend targeted strategies to improve her literacy.	The SALT can provide a school-based social skills group to improve Chloe's understanding of social situations. The community nurse or GP will monitor the medication needed to support Chloe's Crohn's disease. The continence nurse will advise on management of continence, and effects of this on hygiene. A dietician may help Chloe to manage her dietary reactions to eczema and recommend foods which reduce the possibility of her becoming agitated when she is hungry. The occupational therapist may evaluate Chloe's sensory processing responses and teach her, and relevant school staff, how to use more appropriate self-regulation strategies.	A support worker may be involved in monitoring Chloe's sleep patterns, recommending strategies to improve this. A social worker may be assigned to support the family in caring for Chloe, links can be given to: • sibling support group • parents' support group. The social worker may link Chloe to a disability support club and/or summer play scheme. Short breaks may also be arranged through social care.

- Strategies to improve Chloe's continence will be implemented across contexts: school, home and leisure.

- The self-regulation strategies introduced to reduce her overt reactions to sensory stimuli will be implemented in the home and school, leading to more appropriate social behaviours. This will reduce Chloe's mum's concerns about her unusual public presentation.

- Improvements in sleeping will benefit the whole family, reducing Chloe's overt reactions caused by sleep deprivation and improving her mum's ability to cope effectively. This will also enable Chloe to be less tired and more attentive in class.

O   Several parties can be involved in monitoring the effects of Crohn's disease. Teaching staff will be able to liaise with the GP/nurse to monitor effects of medication as she grows.

O   The strategies that Chloe has been introduced to in the social skills group can be facilitated in a number of environments: school, play and home.

O   The dietician can provide dietary advice that will help Chloe manage her extreme reactions to hunger at home, at school and within social contexts.

O   The encouragement to join social groups and play schemes can extend Chloe's social network so that she can continue her shared conversations at school and home.

Group activity: Multi-faceted analysis of need (pages 60–61)

Independent activity	Context
Matthew is able to write the letters of the alphabet (albeit slowly).	Matthew lives with his parents and one-year-old sister. As his family have recently moved north, their friends and extended family are all in the south of England.
Matthew can operate an expanded keyboard independently to type a short sentence.	Matthew's family is sometimes confused by the involvement of a wide range of agencies and different professions.
Matthew can read independently and loves reading.	
Matthew can help to dress and undress himself.	Matthew has a new teacher with a limited understanding of physical disability.

Body structure and functions	Environment
Matthew is a 10-year-old child with athetoid cerebral palsy with dystonic features.	
Matthew has some voluntary control of one arm and is able to assist with some activities such as eating and dressing.	Matthew struggles to pay attention when the class is noisy.
Mathew's ability to engage in play is limited by his lack of stability and voluntary movement.	Matthew is unable to access the PE changing rooms due to the narrow entrance.
Matthew is not able to walk or stand independently and has supported seating, a standing frame and a buggy.	

Personal factors	Participation
Matthew is a bright, responsive child able to indicate his needs (non-verbally).	Matthew has a TA who is with him throughout the school day.
Matthew has a wicked sense of humour and often types rude jokes into his communication aid.	Matthew would like to make friends but is restricted by his limited verbal skills.
Matthew is happy at school.	Matthew uses a communication aid although his motor skills make this slow.
Matthew has a 'girlfriend' who travels in the taxi with him to school.	

Answers to this activity are not definitive, and certain statements may fit several categories. For example, the statement 'Matthew's ability to engage in play is limited by his lack of stability and voluntary movement' could fit into the section 'Body structure and functions' or 'Participation'.

The purpose of this exercise is to reflect the variables which are impacting on Matthew's ability to learn. Outcomes can then be defined under specific headings:

Independent activity

- Needs to improve touch-typing skills.
- Improve speed of dressing/undressing before and after PE.

Participation

- Improve social interaction, reducing the need for adult support.
- Review mechanism for operating communication aid (i.e. sound-activated or eye-controlled switching).

Environment

- Plan to adapting entrance to PE changing rooms.
- Review noise levels in classroom.

Context

- Enable the class teacher to attend CPD training regarding cerebral palsy.
- Refer the family to the local offer site to access local support services.

REFERENCES

Barnett WS (2011). Effectiveness of early educational intervention. *Science*, 333 (6045): 975-978.

Bejerot S, Edgar J & Humble MB (2011). Poor performance in physical education: A risk factor for bully victimization. A case-control study. *Acta Paediatrica*, 100: 413–419.

Boyle C (2013). Labelling in special education: Where do the benefits lie? In A. Holliman (Ed.) *Educational psychology: An international perspective*. London. Routledge.

Breckon J (2014). Tried and tested: How schools can learn lessons from evidence-based research. *The Guardian*, 23 April 2014.

Bruder MB (2010). Early childhood intervention: A promise to children and families for their future. *Exceptional Children*, 76 (3): 339–355.

Campbell WN, Missiuna C & Vaillancourt T (2012). Peer victimization and depression in children with and without motor coordination difficulties. *Psychology in the Schools*, 49 (4): 328–341.

Care Act (2014). London. HMSO.

Childrens Act (1989). London. HMSO.

Children and Families Act (2014). London. HMSO.

Chronically Sick and Disabled Persons Act (1970). London. HMSO.

Community Care (Direct Payments) Act (1996). London. HMSO.

Council for Disabled Children (2008). Inclusion Policy. London. NCB.

Council for Disabled Children (2012). Briefing note on the local offer. http://www.councilfordisabledchildren.org.uk/media/246954/local%20offer.pdf

Council for Disabled Children (2013). School funding changes and children with SEN in mainstream schools: A briefing for parents. Accessed online http://www.councilfordisabledchildren.org.uk/media/408368/cdc_funding_briefing_for_parents.pdf

Dåderman AM, Meurling AW & Levander S (2012). 'Speedy action over goal orientation': Cognitive impulsivity in male forensic patients with dyslexia. *Dyslexia*, 18: 226–235.

deOliveira RF & Wann JP (2011). Driving skills of young adults with developmental coordination disorder: Regulating speed and coping with distraction. *Research in Developmental Disabilities*, 32 (4): 1301–1308.

Department for Business, Innovation and Skills (2014). The Government's strategy to support workforce excellence in further education. London. HMSO.

Department for Children, Schools and Families (2008). (The Bercow Report) A review of services for children and young people (0–19) with speech, language and communication needs. Nottingham. DCSF.

Department for Children, Schools and Families (2009a). Lamb Inquiry: Special educational needs and parental confidence. London. DCSF.

Department for Children, Schools and Families (2009b). Identifying and teaching children and young people with dyslexia and literacy difficulties. Nottingham. DCSF.

Department for Children, Schools and Families (2010). Salt Review: Independent review of teacher supply for pupils with severe, profound and multiple learning difficulties (SLD and PMLD). Nottingham. DCSF.

Department for Education and Skills (1989). The National Curriculum for England and Wales. London. DfES.

Department for Education and Skills (2001). Special education needs: Code of practice. London. DfES.

Department for Education and Skills (2006). Independent review of the teaching of early reading. London. DfES.

Department for Education (2009). Statistical bulletin: Youth cohort study and longitudinal study of young people in England: The activities and experiences of 18 year olds: England 2009 (YCS and LSYPE). http://www.education.gov.uk/rsgateway/DB/SBU/b000937/index.shtml

Department for Education (2011a). Support and aspiration: A new approach to special educational needs and disability: Consultation. London. HMSO.

Department for Education (2011b). UK resilience programme evaluation: Final report. London. HMSO.

Department for Education (2012). School funding reform: Next steps towards a fairer system. London. HMSO.

Department for Education (2013a). Children with special educational needs 2013: An analysis. SFR 42/2013. 23 October 2013. London. DfE.

Department for Education (2013b). Data pack: Improving permanence for looked after children. 9 September 2013. London. DfE.

Department for Education (2013c). Outcomes for children looked after by local authorities in England, as at 31 March 2013. SFR 50/2013. London. DfE.

Department for Education (2013d). Post-16 work experience as a part of 16 to 19 study programmes. London. HMSO.

Department for Education (2013e). Working together to safeguard children. London. HMSO.

Department for Education (2014a). Pupil premium 2014 to 2015: Conditions of grant. February 2014. London. HMSO

Department for Education (2014b). Special educational needs and disability: Research priorities and questions. London. HMSO.

Department for Education (2014c). Increasing options and improving provision for children with special educational needs (SEN). London. HMSO.

Department for Education (2014d). SEND pathfinder programme evaluation: Education health and care planning pathway. London. HMSO.

Department for Education and Department of Health (2014). Special educational needs (SEN) code of practice and regulations. London. HMSO.

Department for Education and Skills (2001). SEN toolkit. London. DfES.

Department for Education and Skills and Department of Health (2006). Joint planning and commissioning framework for children, young people and maternity services. London. HMSO.

Department of Health (2009). Guidance on direct payments for community care, services for carers and children's services. London. HMSO.

Disability Discrimination Act (1995). London. HMSO.

Dunn LM (1968). Special education for the mildly retarded – is much of it justifiable? *Exceptional Children*, 35 (1): 5–22.

Education Act (1944). London. HMSO.

Education (Handicapped Children) Act (1970). London. HMSO.

Education Act (1981). London. HMSO.

Education Act (1996). London. HMSO.

Equality Act (2010). London. HMSO.

Fawcett AJ, Lee R & Nicolson R (2014). Sustained benefits of a multi-skill intervention for pre-school children at risk of literacy difficulties. *Asia Pacific Journal of Developmental Differences*, 1 (1): 62–77.

Fegran L, Hall EOC, Uhrenfeldt L et al. (2013). Adolescents' and young adults' transition experiences when transferring from paediatric to adult care: A qualitative metasynthesis. *International Journal of Nursing Studies,* 51: 123–135.

Flynn F (2008). Experts reveal what they look for in an application. *TES.* 3 January 2013.

Frederickson N & Cline T (2009). Special educational needs, inclusion and diversity. Berkshire. Open University.

Fricke S, Bowyer-Crane C, Haley AJ, Hulme C & Snowling MJ (2013). Efficacy of language intervention in the early years. *Journal of Child Psychology and Psychiatry*, 54: 280–290.

Goldacre B (2013). Building evidence into education. London. DfE.

Gordon (2012). Diabetes transition – assessment of current best practice and development of a future work programme to improve transition processes for young people. http://www.chimat.org.uk/resource/item.aspx?RID=139386

Gheera M (2012). Direct payments and personal budgets for social care. Social Policy Section. London. HMSO.

Guralnick MJ (2011). Why early intervention works. *Infants and Young Children*, 24 (1): 6–28.

Graziano PA, Slavec J, Hart K, Garcia A & Pelham WE (2014). Improving school readiness in preschoolers with behavior problems: Results from a summer treatment program. *Journal of Psychopathology and Behavioral Assessment.* http://link.springer.com/article/10.1007%2Fs10862-014-9418-1

Health and Social Care Act (2012). London. HMSO.

House of Commons Defence Committee (2013). The Armed Forces Covenant in action? Part 3: Educating the children of service personnel. London HMSO

In Control (2014). Briefing: Personal budgets and the school day. http://www.in-control.org.uk/what-we-do/children-and-young-people/publications/children's-programme-publications/briefing-personal-budgets-and-the-school-day.aspx

James H (2014). The right to learn-post 16. *SEN Magazine*, 21 June 2014.

Kilsby M & Beyer S (2011). A financial cost: benefit analysis of Kent Supported Employment: A framework for analysis. Kent County Council.

Koegel LK, Koegel RL, Ashbaugh K & Bradshaw J (2014). The importance of early identification and intervention for children with or at risk for autism spectrum disorders. *International Journal of Speech and Language Pathology*, 16, (1): 50–56.

Lamb B (2013). How will accountability work in the new SEND legislative system? *Journal of Research in Special Educational Needs.* doi: 10.1111/1471-3802.12026

Law Commission (2011). Adult Social Care. London. HMSO.

Lewis J, Mooney A, Brady L-M et al (2010). Special educational needs and disability: Understanding local variation in prevalence, service provision and support. London. HMSO.

Local Government Ombudsman (2014). Ombudsman calls for fair treatment of children with SEN. 4 March 2014. www.lgo.org.uk/news/2014/mar/ombudsman-calls-fair-treatment-children-sen/

Logan SW, Robinson E, Wilson AE& Lucas WA (2012). Getting the fundamentals of movement: A meta-analysis of the effectiveness of motor skill interventions in children. *Child: Care, Health and Development,* 38: 305–315.

Macdonald SJ (2012a). Biographical pathways into criminality: Understanding the relationship between dyslexia and educational disengagement. *Disability & Society.* 27 (3): 427–440.

Macdonald SJ (2012b). "Journey's end": Statistical pathways into offending for adults with specific learning difficulties. *Journal of Learning Disabilities and Offending Behaviour,* 3 (2): 85–97.

Mackey S & McQueen J (1998). Exploring the association between integrated therapy and inclusive education. *British Journal of Special Education.* 25 (1): 22–27.

McCabe PC & Altamura M (2011). Empirically valid strategies to improve social and emotional competence of preschool children. *Psychology in the Schools,* 48 (5): 513–540.

Merriam G (2010). Rehabilitating Aristotle: A virtue ethics approach to disability and human flourishing. *Philosophy and Medicine,* 104: 133–151.

Nalavany BA, Carawan LW & Rennick RA (2010). Psychosocial experiences associated with confirmed and self-identified dyslexia: A participant-driven concept map of adult perspectives. *Journal of Learning Disabilities.* 44 (1): 63–79.

National Health Service Act (1946). London. HMSO.

National Assistance Act (1948). London. HMSO.

National Association of Head Teachers (2014). Changes to the SEN framework: What do school leaders need to know? 25 February 2014. www.naht.org.uk

Norwich B (2014). How does the capability approach address current issues in special educational needs, disability and inclusive education field? *Journal of Research in Special Educational Needs.* 14 (1): 16–21.

Ofsted (2010). The special educational needs and disability review: A statement is not enough. Manchester. HMSO.

Ofsted (2011). Progression post-16 for learners with learning difficulties and/or disabilities. Manchester. HMSO.

Policy Consortium (2014). Taking the pulse of further education. The great FE and skills survey of 2014. http://policyconsortium.co.uk/wp/wp-content/uploads/2014/04/PolicyConsortiumFESurveyReportV1.0LowRes20140430.pdf

Polišenská K & Kapalková S (2014). Language profiles in children with Down Syndrome and children with language impairment: Implications for early intervention. *Research in Developmental Disabilities.* 35 (2): 373–382.

Poor Law Act (1930). London. HMSO.

Praet M & Desoete A (2014). Enhancing young children's arithmetic skills through non-intensive, computerised kindergarten interventions: A randomised controlled study. *Teaching and Teacher Education.* 39: 56–65.

Special Educational Needs and Disability Act (2001). London. HMSO.

Snell J (2011). Employment prospects for young people with learning disabilities. *The Guardian.* 13 April 2011.

Snowling MJ & Hulme C (2012). Interventions for children's language and literacy difficulties. *International Journal of Language and Communication Disorders,* 47 (1): 27–34.

Spivack R, Craston M, Thom G & Carr C (2014). Thematic Report: The education, health and care (EHC) planning pathway for families that are new to the SEN system. London. DfE.

Stevens C (2012). By labelling so many children as 'special needs', we betray those who really do need help. *Mail Online.* 15 May 2012.

Sullivan PM & Knutson JF (2000). Maltreatment and disabilities: A population-based epidemiological study. *Child Abuse and Neglect,* 24 (10): 1257–1273.

Tarling R & Adams M (2010). Summer arts college outcomes report 2007–10. London. Unitas. Available at: http://www.unitas.uk.net/Assets/258207/

The National Health Service (Direct Payments) (Repeal of Pilot Schemes Limitation) Order (2013). London. HMSO.

The Norwood Report (1943). Curriculum and Examinations in Secondary Schools. London. HMSO.

The Special Educational Needs (Personal Budgets) Regulations (2014). London. HMSO.

The Special Educational Needs and Disability Regulations (2014). London. HMSO.

Warnock Committee (1978). Special educational needs: The Warnock Report. London. HMSO.

Warnock M (2005). Special educational needs: a new look. *Impact No.11.* Philosophy of Education Society of Great Britain.

Warnock M (2008). Baroness Warnock: Has inclusion gone too far? *Special Children.* June/July, 14–17.

Webster R (2014). Relying on teaching assistant support for SEN students is a false economy. *The Guardian.* 17 April 2014.

Webster R& Blatchford P (2014). Worlds apart? The nature and quality of the educational experiences of pupils with a Statement for special educational needs in mainstream primary schools. *British Education Research Journal,* published online 21 April 2014.

Williams ED, Tillin T, Whincup P, Forouhi NG & Chaturvedi N (2012). Ethnic differences in disability prevalence and their determinants studied over a 20-year period: A cohort study. *PLoS ONE,* 7 (9): e45602.

Wilson PH, Ruddock S, Smits-Engelsman B, Polatajko H & Blank R (2013). Understanding performance deficits in developmental coordination disorder: A meta-analysis of recent research. *Developmental Medicine & Child Neurology,* 55: 217–228.

World Health Organization (2007). *The International Classification of Functioning, Disability and Health for Children and Youth.* Switzerland. WHO.

Ziviani J, Feeney R, Rodger S & Watter P (2010). Systematic review of early intervention programmes for children from birth to nine years who have a physical disability. *Australian Occupational Therapy Journal,* 57: 210–223.